Beat the Bard

What's Your
Shakespeare IQ?

Joyce E. Henry, Ph.D.

CITADEL PRESS
Kensington Publishing Corp.
www.kensingtonbooks.com

CITADEL PRESS BOOKS are published by

Kensington Publishing Corp.
850 Third Avenue
New York, NY 10022

Copyright © 2003 Joyce E. Henry

All Kensington titles, imprints, and distributed lines are available at special quantity discounts for bulk purchases for sales promotions, premiums, fund-raising, educational, or institutional use. Special book excerpts or customized printings can also be created to fit specific needs. For details, write or phone the office of the Kensington special sales manager: Kensington Publishing Corp., 850 Third Avenue, New York, NY 10022, attn: Special Sales Department; phone 1-800-221-2647.

CITADEL PRESS and the Citadel logo are Reg. U.S. Pat. & TM Off.

First Printing: October 2003

10 9 8 7 6 5 4 3 2 1

Printed in the United States of America

Designed by Leonard Telesca

Library of Congress Control Number: 2003106146

ISBN 0-8065-2509-6

Contents

Prologue

You find Shakespeare intimidating? And you don't know anything about him or his plays? In troth, as Will might have said, you probably know more about him than you think. Shakespeare is all around us—in the words and idioms of our language, in ads for cars, in titles of books and plays, in real estate developments, in newspaper editorials and comic strips. And certainly on shelf after shelf of books in the library.

But know thou this: Shakespeare did not sit down at his tavern bench and declare, "Now I'll write a classic. This afternoon I'll write the greatest play in the English language!" More likely he thought, "What can I come up with that'll keep Dick Burbage happy for another week?" or "How can I create a scene for Will Kempe in this play because audiences think he's so funny?"

Shakespeare wrote for specific actors and to a specific audience. He was a popular author and did not know he was writing for posterity. He thought so little about his future reputation, he made no effort to see his plays published. Nevertheless, the craftsmanship of his plays attests to the care he felt for his work, the language, the motivations of his characters and their theatrical effectiveness.

Beat the Bard is divided into five sections, roughly following Shakespeare's development as a playwright, as well as the divisions of the acts of a play, and perhaps your sophistication as a student of Shakespeare.

The first act, "Amateurs," invites you to test your basic knowledge about the plays that you probably encountered first. The second, "Apprentices," moves you into Shakespeare's apprenticeship, with quizzes on plays he wrote when he first went down to London from Stratford-upon-Avon in the early- and mid-1590s. The third act, "Professionals," corresponds to a still-developing period in Shakespeare's career, when, as a working professional, he honed and polished his skills as a playwright.

By the fourth act, "Major Players," Shakespeare is a major player creating his greatest plays, and you're a Major Player, too, if you've been traveling with him. The last act, "Superstars," is the most difficult section, because although Shakespeare can lean back with his laurels a little, you have to demonstrate your thorough understanding of all his works and their connections.

So give it a whirl! Because he's a lot like us, Shakespeare would enjoy this contest. If you don't beat him the first time around, try again. Have fun!

Some Bard Beaters were helpful in putting these quizzes together; in particular, Professors Louis A. DeCatur, Rebecca Jaroff, and Lois Potter, as well as TV producer Peter Jaroff, project manager Traci Canning, and environmentalist Steve Sandstrom. And, of course, the super Bardolator, Robert Shuman.

The editions used were *The Complete Works of Shakespeare* edited by Hardin Craig and David Bevington (Scott, Foresman, 1973), and *The Two Noble Kinsmen,* edited by Lois Potter (The Arden Shakespeare, 1997). Line numbers will differ in other editions.

Beat the Bard

ACT I

Amateurs

Like actors, amateurs are those who possess passion for a subject, an enthusiasm that has little to do with skill or knowledge or desire for remuneration. Like actors, they are aficionados and sometimes fanatics, and strong supporters of the arts, the sciences, and literature. They embrace every significant, innovative, or foolhardy endeavor and are always willing to learn more. The first section is directed at amateurs who love Shakespeare, have read some of the plays, and have seen a few productions and films. In a sense, we are all amateurs.

Consider section one as a tryout, an audition. It begins with familiar quotations by characters in plays first encountered onstage or in film, for example, *Romeo and Juliet, As You Like It, Othello, Julius Caesar, Twelfth Night, Hamlet, Macbeth, The Merchant of Venice,* even *King Lear.* Although you may not be familiar with the play, you may recognize the quotation—and you have choices to help out. Can anyone not identify the speaker of "To be or not to be"? (You've already gained a point!) Section two moves to ways these characters behave in the context of the plays. Section three focuses upon Shakespeare's life and family, historical facts which you may know; Section four moves to questions about his theater, and Section five ends with questions about his language and poetry. Try them all!

Thereafter "Amateurs" deals with five plays selected for their familiarity: *Romeo and Juliet, A Midsummer Night's Dream, Julius Caesar, As You Like It,* and *Macbeth.* You may find most of the section fairly simple, but one or two questions are a little tricky, so watch out. There are 112 questions altogether; if you answer 57 or more correctly, you are probably at the Professional level. The answers begin on page 25.

Tryouts

I. Which character speaks these well-known lines?

1. "What's in a name? That which we call a rose
   By any other name would smell as sweet."

   a. Rosaline
   b. Juliet
   c. Mariana

2. "The quality of mercy is not strain'd."

   a. Juliet
   b. Desdemona
   c. Portia

3. "All the world's a stage;
   And all the men and women merely players."

   a. Jaques
   b. Orlando
   c. Hamlet

4. "Who steals my purse steals trash."

   a. Hamlet
   b. Macbeth
   c. Iago

5. "Friends, Romans, countrymen, lend me your ears."

   a. Julius Caesar
   b. Mark Antony
   c. Brutus

6. "O, she doth teach the torches to burn bright!"

   a. Romeo
   b. Valentine
   c. Benvolio

7. "To be or not to be; that is the question."

   a. Romeo
   b. Macbeth
   c. Hamlet

8. "If music be the food of love, play on."

   a. Orsino
   b. Jaques
   c. Romeo

9. "O, what a noble mind is here o'erthrown:
   The courtier's, soldier's, scholar's, eye, tongue, sword:
   The expectancy and rose of the fair state."

   a. Horatio
   b. Ophelia
   c. Gertrude

10. "Tomorrow, and tomorrow, and tomorrow,
Creeps in this petty pace from day to day
To the last syllable of recorded time"

   a. Macbeth
   b. Julius Caesar
   c. Hamlet

11. "O, I am fortune's fool!"

   a. Orlando
   b. Romeo
   c. Hamlet

12. "Men have died from time to time, and worms have eaten
them, but not for love."

   a. Beatrice
   b. Kate
   c. Rosalind

   II. Shakespeare's characters behave in unusual ways and
have unusual things done to them. Added to the mix in this
section are a few more plays: *Richard III, A Midsummer Night's
Dream, Much Ado About Nothing,* and *Antony and Cleopatra,*
but don't let anxiety creep in; you probably know most of these.

13. He leaves poetry on trees.

   a. Benedick
   b. Antipholus
   c. Orlando

14. He is tricked by a forged love letter.

   a. Romeo
   b. Malvolio
   c. Bassanio

15. He is drowned in a "malmsey butt."

    a. Clarence
    b. Edward
    c. Richard

16. She is strangled in her bed.

    a. Desdemona
    b. Hermione
    c. Lady Macduff

17. He is stabbed with a poisoned sword.

    a. Richard III
    b. Henry IV
    c. Hamlet

18. She commits suicide with an asp.

    a. Katherine
    b. Emilia
    c. Cleopatra

19. She is rejected at the altar.

    a. Katherine
    b. Hero
    c. Celia

20. He is turned into an ass.

    a. Bottom
    b. Dogberry
    c. Launce

21. He takes poison.

    a. Macbeth
    b. Richard III
    c. Romeo

22. He bungles his suicide.

    a. Othello
    b. Antony
    c. Lear

    III. Now try out some facts you know about Shakespeare's life and family.

23. Shakespeare lived from

    a. 1492 to 1530
    b. 1564 to 1616
    c. 1920 to 1980

24. He grew up in

    a. Stratford-upon-Avon
    b. London
    c. Yorkshire

25. His mother's name was

    a. Anne Hathaway
    b. Mary Arden
    c. Juliet Capulet

26. His father was a

    a. glover
    b. farmer
    c. preacher

27. His wife's name was

    a. Anne Hathaway
    b. Mary Arden
    c. Juliet Capulet

28. They had

    a. one child
    b. two children
    c. three children

29. Their child who died was

    a. Susanna
    b. Judith
    c. Hamnet

30. Legend says that Shakespeare poached deer on the estate of

    a. the earl of Southampton
    b. Sir Richard Cheney
    c. Sir Thomas Lucy

31. Shakespeare's principal company from 1594 to 1601 was known as

    a. the Lord Chamberlain's Men
    b. the Queen's Men
    c. Lord Essex's Men

32. Shakespeare is buried in

    a. Stratford-upon-Avon
    b. Westminster Abbey
    c. Southwark Cathedral

IV. Now identify these facets of the Elizabethan Theater.

33. The theater Shakespeare was most associated with was

   a. the Rose
   b. Covent Garden
   c. the Globe

34. Another theater Shakespeare participated in was

   a. the Blackfriars
   b. the Rose
   c. Covent Garden

35. The "tiring house" in the theater was

   a. the concession stand
   b. the rest room
   c. the dressing room

36. The "groundlings" refers to

   a. apprentice actors
   b. common people who stood for performances
   c. the musicians

37. The "galleries" were spaces reserved for

   a. the highest-paying customers
   b. men without their wives
   c. men with their wives

V. You certainly know something about Shakespeare's language and poetry, but you might get tripped up on one or two of these.

38. Shakespeare wrote in

    a. Old English
    b. Middle English
    c. Early Modern English

39. It's easy to forget that iambic pentameter refers to

    a. a line of five poetic feet of unstressed and stressed syllables
    b. a line of five poetic feet of stressed and unstressed syllables
    c. a line of five poetic feet of stressed and stressed syllables

40. An example of an oxymoron is

    a. "You starveling, you elf-skin, you dried neat's tongue!"
    b. "A woman moved is like a fountain troubled"
    c. "O brawling love! O loving hate!"

41. Unlike the Petrarchan sonnet, the Shakespearean sonnet has

    a. two stanzas of six lines ending with a rhymed couplet
    b. three stanzas of four lines ending plus a rhymed couplet
    c. two four line stanzas and one of six

The connotations of some English words have changed through the centuries. Can you figure out how the italic words in these lines were used?

42. When Hamlet, grieving for his father's death and disgusted with his mother's marrying Claudius, says, "A beast that *wants* discourse of reason would have mourned longer," *wants* means

    a. desires
    b. needs
    c. lacks

43. In *The Taming of the Shrew,* when Kate counsels her female audience to "vail your stomachs, for it is no *boot,*" *boot* means

    a. matter
    b. profit
    c. shoe

44. In King Lear's recognition that he is " a very foolish, *fond* old man," *fond* means

    a. loving
    b. weakened
    c. doting

45. When Hamlet snidely remarks to Claudius that he, Hamlet, is "a little more than kin, and less than *kind,*" *kind* means

    a. loving
    b. natural
    c. animal

46. In explaining his courtship of Desdemona, Othello says, "Upon this *hint* I spake," *hint* means

    a. opportunity
    b. suggestion
    c. invitation

47. In the line, "Tell me, where is *fancy* bred?" from Feste's song in *Twelfth Night, fancy* means

    a. fantasy
    b. elaborateness
    c. love

Did you get tripped up anywhere or did you waltz right through those tryout questions?

Now move on to five specific plays: *Romeo and Juliet, A Midsummer Night's Dream, Julius Caesar, As You Like It,* and *Macbeth.* One or more of these plays is generally foisted upon students at some time during their high school careers, and this section may evoke memories for you of those halcyon (or hideous) days.

Romeo and Juliet

For many people *Romeo and Juliet* is their first close encounter with Shakespeare. And it's a good introduction. The young lovers are appealing, the parents are insensitive, and the Chorus tells the entire plot in the Prologue. What's not to like?

48. The play is set in

    a. Rome
    b. Florence
    c. Verona

49. The Montagues and Capulets are feuding because

    a. three generations ago a Montague killed a Capulet for no good reason
    b. they've feuded as long as anyone can remember
    c. the Capulets have a larger castle

50. According to the text, Romeo first sees Juliet

    a. in church, lighting a candle to the Virgin Mary
    b. sitting in the garden eating an apple
    c. at a ball given by her father

51. "A plague on both your houses!" is spoken by

    a. the Nurse, in the piazza, when the young men make fun of her
    b. Mercutio, as he lies dying from a wound from Tybalt
    c. Benvolio, Romeo's dearest friend, in disgust, after both Tybalt and Mercutio are killed

52. Susan is

    a. the Nurse's dead daughter
    b. Juliet's dead sister
    c. Juliet's mother

53. Juliet's father wants her to marry

    a. Benvolio, because he's such a serious boy
    b. Paris, because he's of noble parentage
    c. Romeo, because that will cement the Capulets' relationship with the Montagues

54. The fiery Tybalt, always spoiling for a fight, is

    a. Juliet's cousin
    b. Romeo's best friend
    c. the Nurse's nephew

55. When Romeo is banished, the Friar's plan for the pair of lovers is for

    a. Romeo and Juliet to flee to Padua, where they can easily take a ship to England and be safe

    b. Romeo to flee to Mantua until the Duke pardons him

    c. Juliet to flee to Mantua to her sympathetic aunt's house

56. The Friar's message to the exiled Romeo does not arrive because

    a. the messenger's horse goes lame

    b. the city is quarantined by plague and no one can enter

    c. the messenger gets the plague

57. When Juliet takes the sleeping potion, she worries about all but one of the following:

    a. the potion will not work

    b. the potion is a poison that the Friar has concocted

    c. she'll wake up too late when Romeo comes and he'll think she's dead

    d. she'll go mad in the vault and play with her forefathers' bones

58. Juliet wakes up from her sleeping potion

    a. too soon

    b. too late

    c. never

59. Statues of Romeo and Juliet in pure gold will be raised over their graves by

    a. the Prince

    b. the Friar

    c. the fathers

60. The play contains three of the four poetic forms below. Which one does not appear?

   a. the sonnet
   b. the aubade
   c. the alexandrine
   d. the epithalamium

61. In Baz Luhrmann's 1996 film, *Romeo and Juliet,* the young lovers pledge their love

   a. in a singles bar
   b. in a swimming pool
   c. at a rave

62. Fill in the missing words in Romeo's speech as he first spies Juliet on her balcony:

   "But, soft! what light through _____ window breaks?
   It is the _____; and Juliet is the _____."

   Did you get half of these questions right? (I know that you're sneaking looks at the answers.) Time to move on to . . .

A Midsummer Night's Dream

   The fairy-tale world of *A Midsummer Night's Dream* continues to delight audiences from kindergarten to senior center in every era. And why not? It celebrates love, youth, music, theater, actors, even the sport of hunting.

63. The setting of the play is

   a. in the English countryside
   b. in and around Athens
   c. in and around Tuscany

64. At the beginning of the play, the wedding of Theseus, the Duke of Athens, and the conquered Hippolyta, Queen of the Amazons, is to occur in

    a. one week
    b. two days
    c. four days

65. If Hermia, who loves Lysander, doesn't marry Demetrius, her father's choice, then

    a. she won't get a dowry
    b. she'll have to become a nun
    c. she'll be banished to Mallorca

66. Lysander, who loves Hermia, suggests they flee

    a. to his aunt's place outside Athens
    b. to a church sanctuary in the woods
    c. to the island of Crete

67. Titania and Oberon, the queen and king of the fairies, quarrel because

    a. she has more fairies than he has
    b. she's been hanging out with Theseus
    c. she has the little Indian boy

68. Puck declares that he will "girdle the earth" in

    a. forty days
    b. forty minutes
    c. four days

69. One of the following flowers is *not* included in Oberon's speech, describing Titania's bower, that begins "I know a bank where the wild thyme blows . . ."

   a. oxlips
   b. violets
   c. clematis
   d. musk roses

70. Today we call the flower with the magic juice in it

   a. lily of the valley
   b. sweet William
   c. pansy

71. In the last act the actors, sometimes called the "mechanicals," perform the play "Pyramus and Thisbe," a tragedy reminiscent of *Romeo and Juliet*. The actors are workingmen, each with a trade. Match the characters with their trades. To help you out (a little), their roles in the play are supplied:

   1. Quince is the director ____   a. bellows-
   2. Snug plays Lion ____   mender
   3. Bottom plays Pyramus ____   b. tailor
   4. Flute plays Thisbe ____   c. carpenter
   5. Snout is Pyramus's father ____   d. tinker
   6. Starveling is Thisbe's mother ____ e. joiner
                                          f. weaver

72. Bottom is transformed into

   a. an ass
   b. a buffalo
   c. a dog

73. Pyramus and Thisbe converse

    a. from the balcony of Theseus's palace
    b. through a fork in the trunk of an oak tree
    c. through a chink in the wall

74. Supply the missing word from Theseus's speech in which he extols the power of the imagination:

    "The lunatic, the lover, and the _____
    Are of imagination all compact"

Now try another play which (like me) you may have studied in the seventh grade.

Julius Caesar

Popular in Shakespeare's day, *Julius Caesar* remains a favorite for its clash of ideals, intrigue, and political shenanigans.

75. Caesar's return to Rome in the first act is a triumph to the common people because

    a. he has invaded England and begun the tower of London
    b. he has invaded Egypt and made love to Cleopatra
    c. he has conquered Pompey at the battle of Pharsalia

76. The holiday being celebrated at the beginning of the play is

    a. the Feast of Lupercal, a festival of February 15
    b. the Saturnalia, a licentious time beginning December 15
    c. the births of Romulus and Remus, the twin boys raised by a wolf who became symbols for Rome

77. Mark Antony offers the crown to Caesar

   a. once, for Rome
   b. twice, because he can't believe Caesar refused it
   c. thrice, to convince the citizens that Caesar is not
      interested in absolute power

78. Caesar is told to "Beware the Ides of March." When is it?

   a. March 1
   b. March 15
   c. March 30

79. "He hath a lean and hungry look," says Caesar, referring to

   a. Cassius
   b. Casca
   c. Brutus

80. Who describes himself as "constant as the northern star"?

   a. Casca
   b. Cassius
   c. Caesar

81. Calpurnia urges Caesar to stay home because

   a. he doesn't pay enough attention to her
   b. she dreamed his statue ran with blood
   c. he's not feeling well

82. In what section of Rome does the assassination of Caesar
   take place?

   a. in the Forum
   b. in Caesar's house
   c. before the Capitol

83. In Caesar's assassination, who strikes the first blow?

    a. Brutus
    b. Casca
    c. Cassius

84. Who strikes the last blow?

    a. Brutus
    b. Casca
    c. Cassius

85. The speech that begins "Friends, Romans, countrymen" is spoken by

    a. Brutus, to the Roman citizens after the fall of Egypt
    b. Mark Antony, to the Roman citizens after the assassination of Caesar
    c. Cicero, to the Roman citizens at the beginning of a speech

86. With whom does Mark Antony join after Caesar's assassination?

    a. Octavius Caesar, Julius's great-nephew
    b. Ligarius, the leader of Sardis
    c. Metellus Cimber, Caesar's henchman

87. The decisive battle between Antony's forces and the conspirators is fought in

    a. Sardis
    b. Liguria
    c. Philippi

88. How does Brutus die?

    a. Mark Antony kills him at the Roman baths
    b. Octavius Caesar kills him in the Tiber
    c. he runs on his own sword

89. Caesar was subject to all of these maladies except

    a. epilepsy
    b. arthritis
    c. fevers
    d. deafness

90. In a famous stage production mounted by Orson Welles in 1937, Caesar was modeled after

    a. Adolf Hitler
    b. Joseph Stalin
    c. Benito Mussolini

As You Like It

A romantic comedy with memorable speeches and the wonderful Rosalind, *As You Like It* has been produced in every era, a joy for all ages.

91. How many brothers does Orlando have?

    a. one
    b. two
    c. none

92. Rosalind and Celia are

    a. sisters
    b. cousins
    c. friends

93. Rosalind, Celia, and Touchstone flee to

    a. an estate in Tuscany
    b. Warwick castle on the Avon
    c. the Forest of Arden

94. Rosalind disguises herself as a man and calls herself

    a. Ganymede, Jupiter's cupbearer
    b. Aliena, the outsider
    c. Cesario, a young knight

95. In the forest of Arden, Rosalind offers to cure Orlando

    a. of his excessive love for her
    b. of his inability to love her
    c. of his melancholy about how badly his brothers have
       treated him

96. The rejected lover of Phoebe the shepherdess is

    a. Lucius
    b. Silvius
    c. Oliver

97. "Omittance is no quittance," which suggests that
    something left out should not be disregarded, is a line
    spoken by

    a. Rosalind
    b. Celia
    c. Phoebe

98. "I can suck melancholy out of a song, as a weasel sucks eggs" is a line spoken by

    a. Duke Senior, in a serious depression after losing his dukedom to his evil brother
    b. Jaques, who is in a serious depression perpetually
    c. Touchstone, who is in a serious depression because he would rather be in court

99. The god who arrives to bless the marriage ceremonies of Rosalind and Orlando and Celia and Oliver is

    a. Bacchus
    b. Pan
    c. Hymen

100. The one character who does not join the happy couples in their return to civilization at the end of the play is

    a. Oliver, Orlando's brother
    b. Jaques, the philosopher
    c. Touchstone, the fool

101. In this famous speech of Duke Senior extolling the pleasures of life in the forest, fill in the missing word in the following quotation:
"Sweet are the uses of _____ ."

    a. exigency
    b. adversity
    c. dependency

Macbeth

Macbeth continues to appeal to audiences with its psychological portraits of a man consumed by ambition and guilt and the powerful woman who influences him.

102. The play is set in

    a. Wales
    b. Scotland
    c. Ireland

103. In the opening, Macbeth and Banquo have just quashed a rebellion by

    a. the Thane of Cawdor and MacDonwald
    b. the Thane of Cawdor and Banquo
    c. the Thane of Cawdor and Malcolm

104. Duncan names as his heir

    a. Malcolm, his older son
    b. Donalbain, his younger son
    c. Macbeth, his victorious thane

105. Relating details of the execution, Malcolm says, "Nothing in his life became him like the leaving it," about

    a. the Thane of Cawdor
    b. Duncan
    c. Banquo

106. The first imaginary object that Macbeth sees is a

    a. cross
    b. dagger
    c. child

107. Lady Macbeth would have murdered Duncan herself except (she says) that

a. someone was coming up the stairs behind her
b. she felt a man should do it
c. he looked like her father as he slept

108. The name of Banquo's son, who escapes the murderers and thus ensures Banquo's posterity, is

a. Frederick
b. Fleance
c. Ferris

109. In the banquet scene, Macbeth gets upset because

a. he thinks the nobles are whispering about him
b. the roast is burned
c. the ghost of Banquo is in his place

110. In act 3, scene 5, the speech of Hecate, the fourth witch, was probably written not by Shakespeare but by

a. Thomas Middleton
b. John Webster
c. John Ford

111. Birnam Wood comes to Dunsinane when

a. a fierce storm uproots all the trees
b. the witches cast a spell
c. the soldiers cut branches to disguise themselves

112. Macbeth is killed by

   a. Malcolm, who throws him over the castle walls
   b. Macduff, who drags the body away and cuts off its
      head
   c. Donalbain, who rips the sword out of Macbeth's
      hands and stabs him in the chest

Answers

Tryouts

I. 1. b. Juliet, *Romeo and Juliet* (II.ii.43–44). On her balcony, Juliet reasons that a name has no real relation to the person who bears it. Romeo would still be Romeo even with another name.

2. c. Portia, *The Merchant of Venice* (IV.i.164). Portia tries to persuade Shylock to release Antonio from his bond of a pound of flesh by arguing that mercy represents the highest form of justice.

3. a. Jaques, *As You Like It* (II.vii.139–140). The cynic Jaques views life simplistically from cradle to grave as a series of theatrical roles.

4. c. Iago, *Othello* (III.iii.157). When Othello demands to know Iago's thoughts, Iago refuses, insinuating that he does not want to tarnish anybody's good name, as a name is more valuable than money.

5. b. Mark Antony, *Julius Caesar* (III.ii.78). Antony eulogizes the murdered Caesar, masterfully refuting Brutus's claim that Caesar was ambitious and wanted more power.

6. a. Romeo, *Romeo and Juliet* (I.v.46). Romeo sees Juliet for the first time, and she blinds him with her radiance.

7. c. This is the beginning of Hamlet's great soliloquy questioning the nature of existence (III.i.56–88).

8. a. Orsino, *Twelfth Night* (I.i.i). The Duke Orsino languishes in his unrequited love for Olivia while listening to music.

9. b. Ophelia, *Hamlet* (III.i.158–60). She laments the Hamlet she used to know, now with his reason "Like sweet bells jangled, out of time and harsh."

10. a. Macbeth, *Macbeth* (V.v.19–21). Life holds no promise for Macbeth; it is tedious and meaningless.

11. b. Romeo, *Romeo and Juliet* (III.i.141). After killing Tybalt, Romeo rails at the unplanned turn events have taken.

12. c. Rosalind, in *As You Like It.* Rosalind tries to make Orlando believe that love is a madness that only fools believe in (IV.i.107–8).

II. 13. c. In *As You Like It,* Orlando, yearning for the love of Rosalind, pins verses on the trees.

14. b. Malvolio, in *Twelfth Night,* is tricked into believing that Olivia loves him, by a forged letter written by Maria.

15. a. Clarence, in *Richard III,* is murdered by being drowned in a vat of malmsey (wine).

16. a. In *Othello,* Desdemona is smothered by Othello in her marriage bed.

17. c. Hamlet is killed by Laertes in their duel with the sword poisoned by Claudius.

18. c. Cleopatra, in *Antony and Cleopatra,* orchestrates her own death with an asp brought to her in a basket.

19. b. Hero, in *Much Ado About Nothing,* is rejected at the altar by Claudio, who believes the false reports of her infidelity.

20. a. In *A Midsummer Night's Dream,* Bottom is metamorphosed into an ass by Oberon, to provide a humiliating love object as punishment for his companion Titania.

21. c. In *Romeo and Juliet,* Romeo, believing Juliet dead, takes poison.

22. b. When Antony, in *Antony and Cleopatra,* believes that Cleopatra is dead, he tries to commit suicide with his sword. He is not immediately successful and suffers a slow and painful death.

III. *Shakespeare's life and family.* 23. b. Shakespeare's birth date is generally considered to be April 23, 1564, since parish records date his christening on April 26, an event traditionally occurring three days after a birth. He died in 1616.

24. a. Shakespeare grew up in Stratford-upon-Avon, a small market town of perhaps two thousand people.

25. b. Mary Arden, Shakespeare's mother, was the daughter of a wealthy landowner in nearby Snitterfield.

26. a. John Shakespeare, William's father, was a prosperous tanner and glover who sold leather goods in his shop; he also dealt in wool, grain, and other farm produce.

27. a. Anne Hathaway, Shakespeare's wife, was eight years his senior and came from Shottery, a short distance from Stratford.

28. c. The Shakespeares had three children: Susanna, born in 1583, and twins, Hamnet and Judith, born in 1585.

29. c. Hamnet died when he was eleven years old.

30. c. A legend survives that Shakespeare poached deer on the nearby estate of Sir Thomas Lucy.

31. a. The Lord Chamberlain's Men was Shakespeare's principal company. Before 1594 there were a number of London

theater companies, several of which Shakespeare might have belonged to. However, after various shufflings due to the plague and patrons' deaths, the Lord Chamberlain's Men, with Shakespeare a prominent member and shareholder emerged in 1594. With the ascension of James I in 1603, the company came to be known as the King's Men.

32. a. Shakespeare's crypt is in Trinity Church, in Stratford-upon-Avon.

IV. *The theater.* 33. c. The Globe was built in about 1599, as a replacement for the Theatre, by Richard and Cuthbert Burbage.

34. a. The Blackfriars was a "private" theater, modeled after the banqueting hall of Tudor mansions. Entrance was more expensive than in the public theater and thus excluded many of the groundlings.

35. c. The "tiring house" was the dressing room for the actors.

36. b. The "groundlings" were those who stood in the pit, the large area in front of the stage at ground level. Today that would be the orchestra section.

37. a. The "galleries" were built in three tiers around the perimeter of the Globe and were the most expensive seats. Today they would be the equivalent of the mezzanine or loge sections.

V. *Facets of Shakespeare's language.* 38. c. Shakespeare's language is Early Modern English. Old English is roughly dated from 450 to 1100, Middle English from 1100 to 1500, and Early Modern English from 1500 to 1800.

39. a. The iambic pentameter line is composed of five feet of unstressed and stressed syllables, e.g., "Thĕ quál | ĭtý | ŏf mér | cў ís | nŏt stráin'd."

40. c. An oxymoron is a phrase that links two usually incompatible or incongruous items. A traditional example is "jumbo shrimp."

41. b. For a good example of a sonnet, see the Prologue to *Romeo and Juliet*.

42. c. In this instance *wants* means "lacks." It does not carry the modern meaning of "desires."

43. b. *Boot* means "profit" or "advantage," something given in addition to the bargain. Think of "booty."

44. c. *Fond* in Shakespeare's time could mean "doting."

45. b. Hamlet means that his relationship to Claudius is unnatural—in other words, that it's weird.

46. a. *Hint* here means "opportunity" rather than suggestion.

47. c. To Elizabethans, *fancy* was applied to amorous inclinations or "love."

Romeo and Juliet

48. c. The play is set in Verona, Italy.

49. b. The Montagues and the Capulets have been feuding as long as anyone can remember, but no one can remember why.

50. c. Romeo first sees Juliet at a ball at her home; although he was not invited, he has attended it, in hopes of seeing his love Rosaline.

51. b. Mercutio speaks these words as he is dying.

52. a. Susan is the Nurse's daughter who was born at the same time as Juliet but died, probably as a baby.

53. b. Juliet's father wants Juliet to marry the county, Paris, because he's from a good family, youthful, and nobly trained.

54. a. Tybalt is Juliet's cousin; he is Lady Capulet's nephew.

55. b. The Friar counsels Romeo to flee to Mantua and then wait until he can announce the marriage, reconcile friends, and get a pardon from the Prince.

56. b. The Friar's message to Romeo in Mantua about Juliet's faked death does not arrive because the plague has broken out and no one can enter the city.

57. c. The one fear Juliet does not express is that she'll wake up too late, and Romeo will think she's dead. Which is what happens.

58. b. Juliet wakes up a few moments too late; Romeo has arrived and, believing that she is dead, kills himself. Had Juliet awakened sooner, the play could have ended differently.

59. c. The fathers, grief-stricken and guilt-ridden, promise to erect statues of gold over the tombs of Romeo and Juliet.

60. c. The play does not contain an alexandrine, a poetic line with six iambic feet. (Remember the iambic foot? Two syllables, one unstressed, one stressed: dah-DAH.) The play does contain the other poetic forms, all integral to the text.

61. b. Yes, in the Luhrmann film the lovers fall into the swimming pool and express their love.

62. Here's Romeo's full speech:

> "But, soft! what light through *yonder* window breaks?
> It is the *east*; and Juliet is the *sun.*"

A Midsummer Night's Dream

63. b. Although the "mechanicals" seem to belong to the English countryside, the play is set in Athens, perhaps because

Athenian law would be stricter concerning the disobedience of a daughter.

64. c. Theseus remarks, "Four happy days bring in / Another moon," presumably the sign for the wedding (I.i.2–3).

65. b. If she doesn't marry Demetrius, Hermia will have to become a nun, "chanting faint hymns to the cold fruitless moon" (I.i.73).

66. a. Lysander's suggestion is that they flee to his aunt's place, seven leagues outside Athens where they would not be subject to Athenian law (I.i.159).

67. c. Titania has cared for the little Indian boy, the son of a dear friend who died. Oberon wants him also.

68. b. Puck says "I'll put a girdle round the earth / In forty minutes" (II.i.75–76).

69. c. The one flower not included in Oberon's speech is the clematis. Oberon says:

> "I know a bank where the wild thyme blows,
> Where oxlips and the nodding violet grows,
> Quite over-canopied with luscious woodbine,
> With sweet musk-roses and with eglantine."
> (II.i.249–252)

70. c. We would call Oberon's special flower the pansy.

71. 1. c. Quince is a carpenter.
    2. e. Snug is a joiner.
    3. f. Bottom is a weaver.
    4. a. Flute is a bellows-mender.
    5. d. Snout is a tinker.
    6. b. Starveling is a tailor.

72. a. Bottom is transformed into an ass, traditionally a stupid and stubborn animal (III.).

73. c. Pyramus and Thisbe converse through a chink in the wall, made possible through the pantomime of Snug the joiner's fingers (V.).

74. The missing word is *poet.* And Shakespeare's luminous speech links the madman, the lover, and the poet-playwright together in the artistry of their imaginations (V.i.7–8).

Julius Caesar

75. c. Caesar has conquered Pompey at the battle of Pharsalia; Pompey was then murdered in Egypt.

76. a. The Feast of Lupercal was celebrated on February 15 of each year. It celebrated fertility for the people, fields, and flocks.

77. c. Mark Antony offers the crown to Caesar thrice.

78. b. In the ancient Roman calendar, the Ides was the fifteenth of March, May, July, and October, and the thirteenth of the other months.

79. a. Thus Caesar describes Cassius (I.ii.194), adding, "He thinks too much: such men are dangerous."

80. c. Caesar says that he is "constant as the northern star" (III.i.60) as he rejects Casca's petition for the enfranchisement of Publius Cimber. He banished Cimber earlier, and he remains constant in this judgment.

81. b. Calpurnia urges Caesar to stay home because she dreamed his statue ran with blood (II.ii.76).

82. c. In Shakespeare's version, Caesar is assassinated before the Capitol, although Plutarch locates the assassination in the portico of Pompey's theater, where the senate was sitting.

83. b. Casca, who is described by Cassius as quick "in execution of any bold or noble enterprise," (I.ii.301) strikes the first blow.

84. a. The last blow is struck by Brutus, evoking Caesar's last words, "et tu, Brute," (III.i.77), meaning "And you too, Brutus?"

85. b. These words begin Mark Antony's powerful funeral oration for Caesar, which persuades the common people to turn against the conspirators, Brutus, Cassius, Casca, and the others (III.ii.77).

86. a. Mark Antony joins with Caesar's nephew, Octavius, and Lepidus, to fight the conspirators.

87. c. Brutus persuades Cassius to leave the safety of the hills around Sardis and to meet Antony and Octavius on the plains of Philippi. A major mistake.

88. c. Brutus runs on his own sword.

89. b. The one ailment that Caesar apparently did not suffer was arthritis.

90. c. Orson Welles modeled his version of Caesar upon Benito Mussolini.

As You Like It

91. b. Orlando has two brothers. Oliver is the oldest; his other brother is Jaques, whom Oliver keeps at school, and who appears only at the very end of the play to announce the conversion of Duke Frederick to a religious life and the renunciation of his lands and crown.

92. b. Rosalind and Celia are cousins; they have grown up together and love each other as sisters.

93. c. When Duke Frederick, Celia's father, banishes Rosalind, Celia and the fool, Touchstone, join her in flight to the Forest of Arden.

94. a. Rosalind takes the name of Ganymede, the cupbearer to Jupiter.

95. a. Rosalind, who is disguised as a man, offers to cure Orlando of his love for her, by pretending to be his love and behaving like a silly woman.

96. b. Phoebe's lover is Silvius, a simple shepherd of the Forest of Arden.

97. c. Phoebe, who fell in love with Rosalind at first sight, says "Omittance is no quittance," meaning that although Rosalind has scorned her, she will not give up her pursuit.

98. b. The line is spoken by Jaques (II.v.12). When the singer Amiens says that if he sings another song, Jaques will grow sad, Jaques is eager to hear it because he loves to wallow in melancholia.

99. c. The god who arrives in the flesh (so to speak) is Hymen, the god of marriage.

100. b. The one character who does not convert at the end of the play is Jaques, who will stay on in the Forest of Arden to study philosophy at the abandoned cave of Duke Senior (V.iv.202).

101. b. "Sweet are the uses of *adversity*" is spoken by Duke Senior (II.1.12) as he explains to his followers that although banished they will find "tongues in trees, books in the running brooks, /Sermons in stones, and good in every thing" (II i.16–17).

Macbeth

102. b. The play is set in Inverness castle in Scotland.

103. a. Macbeth and Banquo have just put down the rebellion of the Thane of Cawdor and MacDonwald.

104. a. Duncan names his older son, Malcolm, as his heir (I.iv.38).

105. a. The Thane of Cawdor, says Ross, died "As one that

had been studied in his death" (I.iv.9). Macbeth is then awarded his title.

106. b. Macbeth sees an imaginary dagger before he kills Duncan (II.i.33).

107. c. Lady Macbeth says, "Had he not resembled/My father as he slept, I had done't" (II.ii.13–14).

108. b. Banquo's son is Fleance, who will carry on Banquo's line, which will produce a series of kings.

109. c. Macbeth sees the ghost of Banquo sitting at the banquet table.

110. a. Scholars generally agree that Hecate's speech (III.v.21–35) was written by Thomas Middleton.

111. c. Birnam Wood comes to Dunsinane when the attacking soldiers camouflage themselves with branches cut from its trees.

112. b. Macbeth is killed by Macduff. Thus the witches' prophecy that he need not fear anyone born of woman is fulfilled, for Macduff was "from his mother's womb/ Untimely ripp'd" (V.viii.15–16).

ACT II

Apprentices

Welcome to the second act of your Shakespearience! If you amassed a score of 85 in the first section, congratulations. But don't get too comfortable, because you've now become an Apprentice, according to the dictionary, one who is "learning the rudiments of a trade, art, or calling under a skilled worker."

Shakespeare himself was an apprentice when he wrote the ten comedies and histories in this section, all before 1599. He was experimenting with subject matter, styles, plots, and language, in other words, learning his craft, referring to authors who had gone before him. You can accompany him in his apprenticeship. In the first scene are the comedies: *The Comedy of Errors,* a new rendering of Plautus's old farce; *The Taming of the Shrew,* developed from folk tales; *The Two Gentlemen of Verona,* his first attempt at romantic comedy; and *Love's Labour's Lost,* a courtly comedy in the style of popular author John Lyly. Next come two early histories, *Richard III* and *Titus Andronicus,* even earlier attempts at tragedy than *Romeo and Juliet.* These are followed by the later histories, *Richard II, 1 Henry IV, 2 Henry IV,* and *Henry V.* I know you're asking, "Why *Richard III* before *Richard II?* Good question. *Richard III* was written before *Richard II* at an even earlier time and is more clearly an apprentice work than the elegant *Richard II.*

(You'll find the answers to all 126 questions beginning on page 67).

> So, the game's afoot!
> Follow your spirit, and upon this charge
> Score, "Ten new quizzes right and Beat the Bard!"

The Early Comedies

The comedies are appealing because of the youth of the lovers, the variety of their courtships, the wit and humor of the clowns, and of course the happy endings. Not surprisingly, all of them have seen life as Broadway musicals.

The Comedy of Errors

The Comedy of Errors directly derives from a Latin farce.

1. At the beginning of the play, the absurd statute that threatens Aegeon's life and frames the plot is that

    a. all Ephesans must shave their heads bald
    b. any Syracusan found in Ephesus will be subject to a fine or death
    c. any Ephesan wanting to marry a Syracusan will be subject to a fine or death

2. Antipholus of Syracuse is in Ephesus because he is looking for

    a. his father, who ducked out on the family after meeting the love of his life
    b. his distraught mother, who disappeared after giving birth to twins
    c. his twin brother, who disappeared during a storm at sea

3. The element that results in all the errors of the comedy is

    a. Luciana has eloped with Antipholus of Syracuse
    b. Aegeon is looking for his wife
    c. there are two sets of twins who are mistaken for one
       another

4. The important prop that complicates the plot is

    a. a handkerchief embroidered with strawberries
    b. a gold ring entwined with grape leaves
    c. a gold chain

5. By act 5, Antipholus of Syracuse is eager to leave Ephesus
    because

    a. he has been dragged off to dine with a woman he's
       never seen before who seems to think she's his wife
    b. a strange merchant gives him a gold chain
    c. he is arrested for being a Syracusan
    d. he is charged with denying possession of the chain
    e. all of the above
    f. all except c

6. By act 5, Dromio of Syracuse is eager to leave Ephesus
    because

    a. he is beaten by his master for inviting him to go home
       to his wife and dinner
    b. he is pursued by the fat and greasy kitchen wench
    c. his master appears to be out of his mind
    d. he secures money to get his master out of jail, and then
       finds him surprisingly free
    e. all except c
    f. all of the above

7. The 1938 Broadway musical adapted by Rodgers and Hart from this play was

   a. *Do Your Own Thing*
   b. *The Boys from Syracuse*
   c. *A Funny Thing Happened on the Way to the Forum*

8. Here are the speakers. Match them to their speeches. When in doubt, guess. Give yourself a point if you get two or more correct.

   a. Dromio of Syracuse   d. Balthasar
   b. Dromio of Ephesus   e. Antipholus of Syracuse
   c. Luciana   f. Abbess

   1. "A man is master of his liberty." ____
   2. "When the sun shines let foolish gnats make sport." ____
   3. "Small cheer and great welcome makes a merry feast." ____
   4. "Time is a very bankrupt and owes more than he's worth to season." ____
   5. "I am an ass indeed; you may prove it by my long ears." ____
   6. "The venom clamours of a jealous woman Poisons more deadly than a mad dog's tooth." ____

The Taming of the Shrew

Sometimes scorned by feminists, *Shrew* continues Shakespeare's experiments; in this instance, he is rewriting folktale material.

9. In the first few lines of the play, what is happening to the tinker, Christopher Sly?

    a. he's making obscene advances to the hostess of the tavern
    b. he's being arrested by the constable for doing the above
    c. he's being thrown out of the tavern for not paying his bill

10. What is the joke played on Sly?

    a. he's told he's the father of three children
    b. he's dressed up and told he's a lord
    c. his friends steal his wallet

11. The city that Petruchio comes from is

    a. Padua
    b. Verona
    c. Florence

12. One of the following is not a suitor of Bianca

    a. Hortensio
    b. Lucentio
    c. Lorenzo
    d. Gremio

13. To woo Bianca, Lucentio disguises himself as

    a. a Latin teacher
    b. a music teacher
    c. a French teacher

14. When Petruchio arrives for his wedding to Katherine, he is dressed in

    a. a white tie and a rose cummerbund
    b. a toga, in imitation of Plato
    c. old pants and boots

15. At the end of the play, Katherine wins Petruchio's wager for him

    a. by serving him his dinner of frogs' feet
    b. by stamping on her hat
    c. by dancing the tarantella

16. Fill in the blanks in the speech below. (If Shakespeare's choices are not coming to mind, fill in your own and count yourself a point for doing so.)

    "I am ashamed that women are so _____
    To offer war when they should _____ for peace."

17. The 1948 musical adapted from this play was called

    a. *Kiss Me, Kate*
    b. *Call Me Madam*
    c. *Miss Saigon*

18. The actors who played Katherine and Petruchio in the 1967 film version directed by Franco Zeffirelli were

    _____ _____

The Two Gentlemen of Verona

19. In act 1, scene 1, Valentine, saying good-bye to his friend Proteus, is off to

    a. Padua
    b. Mantua
    c. Milan

20. The reason he's going is to

    a. pursue love, which has eluded him so far in his hometown
    b. acquire honor, a necessity for every red-blooded young man
    c. find a lucrative profession

21. The lines " . . . he cannot be a perfect man,
    Not being tried and tutor'd in the world"
    are spoken by

    a. the Duke
    b. Proteus
    c. Don Antonio

22. Proteus betrays his friend Valentine by

    a. trying to woo Sylvia, the girl Valentine loves
    b. accusing him of stealing the Duke's coffers
    c. forging his name on a letter slandering Sylvia

23. Sylvia gives Proteus

    a. a book of romantic poems
    b. her picture
    c. a ring that belonged to her grandmother

24. Launce's dog is called

   a. Buddy
   b. Spot
   c. Crab

25. The rope ladder is supposed to be used

   a. to escape to the tree house
   b. to reach an underground tunnel
   c. to rescue Sylvia from the bedroom where her father has
      locked her in

26. To pursue Valentine, Julia

   a. puts on male attire
   b. hires a carriage and driver
   c. speaks with a German accent

27. The comic actor in Shakespeare's company who would
    have played Launce was

   a. Will Kempe
   b. Robert Armin
   c. Richard Burbage

28. The rock musical based on *The Two Gentleman of Verona*
    was performed in

   a. the 1970s
   b. the 1980s
   c. the 1990s

Love's Labor's Lost

29. The poetic device Shakespeare uses in the title *Love's Labor's Lost* is

    a. onomatopoeia
    b. doggerel
    c. alliteration

30. The setting of the play is in

    a. France, near Versailles
    b. a palatial villa in Tuscany
    c. northwest Spain, in a city known today for the running of the bulls

31. The ill-advised vow that the prince and his friends make is

    a. to seek the Holy Grail in Istanbul
    b. to drink no beer for three years
    c. to study for three years and not pursue women

32. The first young man to break the vow is

    a. the King
    b. Dumayne
    c. Longaville
    d. Berowne

33. The last young man to break the vow is

    a. the King
    b. Dumayne
    c. Longaville
    d. Berowne

34. The profession of the satirical character Holofernes is

    a. pedant
    b. steward
    c. preacher

35. The "entertainment" that the young men devise for their ladies includes their disguising themselves as

    a. Muscovites, in Russian habits
    b. Esquimaux, in furs and animal tusks
    c. Druids painted blue

36. The Princess is compelled to leave at the end of the play because

    a. she's bored to death by these fellows
    b. she's been insulted
    c. she's had distressing news

37. The task Rosaline imposes upon Berowne if he wishes to win her is

    a. to cheer up those in hospitals for a year
    b. to avoid speaking to another woman for a year
    c. to learn to speak French fluently

38. In 2000, a musical film adaptation of the play was produced by

    a. Steven Spielberg
    b. Franco Zeffirelli
    c. Kenneth Branagh

The Early History Plays

You've had your fun—now get serious. In these early history plays, Shakespeare is still learning how to develop character; and like the study of acting, it doesn't always happen overnight.

Richard III

Richard III is a play full of wicked fascination for both audiences and actors.

39. True or False:

    a. The red rose symbolizes the House of Lancaster, the white rose the House of York. _____
    b. Richard III belongs to the House of York. _____

40. Richard's opening soliloquy, which begins

> "Now is the winter of our discontent
> Made glorious summer by this sun of York"

is a good example of

    a. irony
    b. satire
    c. parody

41. The infirmities that Richard suffers include all but

    a. a crook'd back
    b. a withered hand
    c. a glass eye

42. In act 1, scene 1, Clarence is on his way to

    a. the court to be knighted for his service to Edward
    b. battle to avenge his father's death
    c. imprisonment in the Tower

43. The token Richard gives to Anne, which she takes, is

    a. his picture in a gold locket
    b. a necklace strung with pearls and diamonds
    c. a ring to signify their relationship

44. Margaret curses everyone except

    a. Edward, Prince of Wales
    b. Elizabeth
    c. Buckingham
    d. Rivers and Dorset

45. Richard and Buckingham have a falling-out because

    a. Buckingham doesn't agree to the murder of the little princes
    b. Buckingham disapproves of Richard's marriage to Anne and would like her for himself
    c. Buckingham would like to make a pilgrimage to the Holy Land to atone for his sins

46. Dighton and Forrest, who are referred to but never appear in the play, are

    a. the two priests who "convince" Richard to take the crown
    b. two men who provide entertainment at the castle
    c. the two murderers of the little princes

47. When Richard sends Stanley to muster troops, he ensures Stanley's loyalty by

    a. holding Stanley's son George hostage
    b. promising Stanley an earldom
    c. threatening Stanley's life if he doesn't bring his men

48. A ghost says, "The first was I that help'd thee to the crown,/The last was I that felt thy tyranny"

    Who is speaking? _____

49. The field of the last battle is

    a. Bosworth
    b. Agincourt
    c. Tewksbury

50. At the end of the play, the man who will take over and become king is

    a. Derby
    b. Stanley
    c. Richmond

Actors of *Richard III*

Richard III is a wonderful role for an actor, since villainy is a joy to create without the consequences that accrue in reality. To help you out here, the list of actors is given alphabetically, but their speeches are offered chronologically.

a. Richard Burbage	f. Edmund Kean
b. Colley Cibber	g. Richard Mansfield
c. Richard Dreyfuss	h. Ian McKellen
d. David Garrick	i. Laurence Olivier
e. Charles Kean	j. Al Pacino

51. I was a friend and sharer with Shakespeare at the Globe, and I also created most of the leading roles, one of which was Richard III. Although I created Hamlet, my colleagues considered Richard my best role, and backstage called me "King Dick."

_____

52. I edited *Richard III*, cutting the entire first act, though interpolating speeches from *3 Henry IV, 2 Henry IV,* and *Henry V.* Since I did not have a very strong voice, I felt that I should limit myself to the villains Shakespeare wrote, which were the best parts anyway. I invented the line "Off with his head; so much for Buckingham," which I understand was used for several centuries.

_____

53. I debuted in London at the Goodman's Fields Theatre in Whitechapel in the role of Richard, where my performance was viewed as "the most extraordinary and great that was ever known on such an occasion." I debuted at Drury Lane the following year again with Richard and played the role in almost every season for the next thirty years. Richard Brinsley Sheridan said my Richard was "firm, but not terrible enough." Mrs. Siddons thereupon protested, "God bless me, what could be more terrible?"

_____

54. I was the son of the actor below, although considered not as good as the old man. When I was performing Richard III in Edinburgh, my Newfoundland dog escaped from my dressing room and, becoming upset during the duel scene, bounded onto the stage. I had to die a voluntary death, Richmond ran off, and my dog stood over me and licked my face. At the conclusion of the play, the audience called for the dog.

_____

55. In my first season at Drury Lane I saved the theater from financial ruin with my Richard. One critic said that the role of Richard allowed me to "show off that tempest and whirlwind of the soul." And Byron said, "By God, he is a soul." Still, after a scandalous affair, I was pelted with cakes and bottles while playing Richard and driven off the stage in Boston in 1825.

_____

56. Although my productions were not particularly successful, I included several innovations. When I took the throne after learning of the murder of the little princes, a red light streamed down through the stained-glass windows, looking like blood falling upon my face and hands. Then I slid from the throne and sat brooding at its feet. In the tent scene, when I awoke from the dream, I thought Catesby another avenging spirit, and in terror made the sign of the cross a number of times, finally touching him to satisfy myself that he was a friend.

_____

57. I took Richard's misshapen body, his long pointed nose, and his sardonic smile, but I wanted to convince the audience of the mind behind the mask. There's something of the flirting, calculating witch about him, so I kept the long black curls to insinuate this femininity.

_____

58. In this film I am an actor hired from California to play Richard. The director tells me that Richard is "the queen who wanted to be king." I try desperately to create the role in this fashion, but the production is a disaster. Still, I get the girl at the end of the flick.

_____

59. I play Richard in early-twentieth-century dress; the opening soliloquy is at a coronation ball which I begin over the microphone as the crowd dances, then move into the men's room. But the best scene is with Lady Anne in the morgue with her dead husband. I pull the ring out of my pocket and put it in my mouth before giving it to her.

_____

60. I feel that Richard is a man alienated from his own body and himself, and is trying to find that self. In my film, I play an actor who is also looking for the inner self of Richard, and I explain the story to the audience as I go through the process of creating a performance.

_____

Titus Andronicus

Apprenticeships aren't always easy, or progress evenly to mastery. There's many a misstep and wrong path taken. Check out another apprentice work of Shakespeare—a gruesome play, largely overlooked and even despised for centuries, but one that evoked some interest with Julie Taymor's 1999 film *Titus.*

61. Titus, returning victorious from the war with the Goths, has contributed the following number of sons to the war effort.

a. five
b. ten
c. fifteen
d. twenty-five

62. The eldest son of the Queen of the Goths is chosen to appease the spirits of Titus's dead sons. He will be

    a. fed to the crocodiles along the Tiber
    b. torn apart by enraged horses
    c. have his hewed limbs and entrails burned in a fire
    d. be crucified like a common criminal

63. After his election as emperor, Saturninus chooses Lavinia to be his queen. This angers her betrothed

    a. Valentine
    b. Bassianus
    c. Marcus

64. Lavinia is stolen away from court by her betrothed, leading to the death of her brother Mutius at the hands of

    a. Titus
    b. Saturninus
    c. Lucius

65. The two brothers, Demetrius and Chiron, quarrel over Lavinia, but Aaron suggests that they

    a. take her in the woods and rape her
    b. win her from Bassianus with poems and sweetmeats
    c. flatter her with tributes from the classical poets

66. During the hunt, Lavinia loses

    a. her chastity
    b. her husband
    c. her hands
    d. her tongue
    e. the bag of gold hidden by Aaron
    f. all of the above
    g. all of the above except *e*

67. Marcus compares Lavinia's rape to that of

    a. Cressida
    b. Daphne
    c. Philomel

68. Bassianus is murdered because

    a. he was insensitive enough to marry Lavinia when the emperor desired her
    b. he witnessed Tamora and Aaron making love in the forest
    c. he was part of Tamora's plan to avenge her son's death
    d. all of the above

69. Part of Tamora's vengeance is to implicate Titus's sons in Bassianus's murder

    a. with a planted letter
    b. with a bloody dagger left in the steaming body of Bassianus
    c. with a rope used to strangle Bassianus and hang him from an elder tree

70. Titus can save his sons, who have been accused of murdering the emperor's brother, if he will

    a. send the emperor a note promising a large ransom
    b. deliver up the mutilated Lavinia to the courts to be tried as a "common stale"
    c. send the emperor his chopped off hand
    d. send the emperor his mutilated genitalia as evidence that he will reproduce no more sons

71. Titus emerges as a tragic hero when he realizes that suffering

    a. is inflicted on man without reason
    b. is imposed on man for his education
    c. promises redemption in the next life

72. To help Titus avenge the deaths of his children

    a. Lavinia will carry his severed hand in her teeth
    b. Titus will carry the severed head of one son, perhaps Martius
    c. Marcus will carry the severed head of another son, perhaps Quintus
    d. Lucius will raise an army of Goths and return to fight his Roman enemies
    e. all of these grotesqueries
    f. *a* and *b* but not *c* and *d*

73. Lavinia identifies her attackers by

    a. pointing her stumps at Demetrius and Chiron at court
    b. locating the story of Philomela in Lucius's book of Ovid
    c. sinking her teeth into the hands of Demetrius and Chiron
    d. writing the names of her attackers in the sand with a stick held in her mouth
    e. *a* and *c* but not *b* and *d*
    f. *b* and *d* but not *a* and *c*

74. The first obvious evidence of Tamora's indiscretion with Aaron is

    a. his garments left behind in her palace room
    b. his hunting gear found in a room where both Tamora and Aaron had spent time
    c. her baby is born black

75. In order to prepare for the final banquet, Titus

    a. cuts the throats of Chiron and Demetrius
    b. grinds their bones to dust and makes a paste with their blood
    c. makes pasties of their heads
    d. bakes their flesh in a pie and serves it to Tamora at the banquet
    e. all of the above
    f. none of the above, because Titus was hoping for a spiritual revenge that would be more horrible

76. At the final banquet, the stage is strewn with the bodies of

    a. Lavinia, because her shame was too great
    b. Tamora, who died after eating the flesh of her two sons
    c. Titus, dressed like a cook, who is killed by the angry emperor
    d. Saturninus, killed by an angry son of Titus
    e. the black baby, offspring of the "irreligious Moor"
    f. Demetrius and Chiron, who underwent a metamorphosis
    g. all of the above except *e* and *f*
    h. all of the above except *e*

Maybe it's a good thing that Shakespeare got that out of his system.

The Histories

Many characters appear in the history plays of the second tetralogy, which begins with *Richard II,* continues with the two parts of *Henry IV* and concludes with *Henry V.*

Wade into the next experiment with the identification of the speakers of these lines. (Note: some speakers are used twice.) If all else fails, try the old process of elimination.

a. Chorus	h. Justice Shallow
b. Falstaff	i. Lady Percy
c. Hal	j. Lord Mowbray
d. Henry IV	k. Richard II
e. Henry V	l. Warwick
f. Hotspur	m. Will
g. John of Gaunt	n. Duke of York

77. "O for a muse of fire, that would ascend
    The brightest heaven of invention,
    A kingdom for a stage, princes to act
    And monarchs to behold the swelling scene!"

    _____

78. "I know you all, and will awhile uphold
    The unyok'd humour of your idleness"

    _____

79. "Do you not love me? do you not, indeed?
    Well, do not then; for since you love me not,
    I will not love myself."

    _____

80. "The language I have learn'd these forty years,
    My native English, now I must forgo:
    And now my tongue's use is to me no more
    Than an unstringed viol or a harp."

    _____

81. "Jesu, Jesu, dead! 'A drew a good bow; and dead! 'A shot a
    fine shoot: John a' Gaunt loved him well, and betted much
    money on his head. Dead! 'A would have clapped i' th' clout
    at twelvescore."

    _____

82. "I have been studying how I may compare
    This prison where I live unto the world:
    And because the world is populous
    And here is not a creature but myself,
    I cannot do it."

    _____

83. "By heaven, methinks it were an easy leap,
    To pluck bright honour from the pale-fac'd moon,
    Or dive into the bottom of the deep,
    Where fathom line could never touch the ground
    And pluck up drowned honour by the locks;
    So he that doth redeem her thence might wear
    Without corrival all her dignities."

    _____

84. "England, bound in with the triumphant sea,
    Whose rocky shore beats back the envious siege
    Of wat'ry Neptune, is now bound in with shame,
    With inky blots and rotten parchment bonds:
    That England, that was wont to conquer others,
    Hath made a shameful conquest of itself."

    _____

85.   "O sleep, O gentle sleep,
      Nature's soft nurse, how have I frighted thee,
      That thou no more wilt weigh my eyelids down
      And steep my senses in forgetfulness?"

      _____

86.   "Tut, tut!
      Grace me no grace, nor uncle me no uncle:
      I am no traitor's uncle; and that word 'grace'
      In an ungracious mouth is but profane."

      _____

87. "There is a history in all men's lives,
      Figuring the nature of the times deceas'd;
      The which observ'd, a man may prophesy,
      With a near aim, of the main chance of things
      As yet not come to life, which in their seeds
      And weak beginning lie intreasured."

      _____

88. "Once more unto the breach, dear friends, once more;
      Or close the wall up with our English dead.
      In peace there's nothing so becomes a man
      As modest stillness and humility;
      But when the blast of war blows in our ears,
      Then imitate the action of the tiger;
      Stiffen the sinews, summon up the blood."

      _____

89. "I am afeard there are few die well that die in a battle; for
      how can they charitably dispose of any thing, when blood
      is their argument? Now, if these men do not die well, it
      will be a black matter for the king that led them to it; who
      to disobey were against all proportion of subjection."

      _____

90. "O my poor kingdom, sick with civil blows!
    When that my care could not withhold thy riots,
    What wilt thou do when riot is thy care?
    O, thou wilt be a wilderness again,
    Peopled with wolves, thy old inhabitants!"

    _____

91. "What is honour? A word. What is in that word honour?
    Air. A trim reckoning. Who hath it? he that died a
    Wednesday. Doth he feel it? no. Doth he hear it? no.
    'Tis insensible then? Yea, to the dead. But will it not live
    with the living? no. Why? detraction will not suffer it.
    Therefore I'll none of it."

    _____

Shakespeare is becoming more skillful, and his experiments are almost over. Consider, for instance . . .

Richard II

92. Richard II is the son of

    a. Richard I
    b. Henry VI
    c. Edward, the Black Prince

93. Richard's character flaws include

    a. extravagance
    b. arbitrariness
    c. religiosity
    d. bad judgments
    e. all of the above
    f. all of the above except *c*

94. Richard stops the contest between Lord Mowbray and Henry Bolingbroke, Duke of Hereford and son to John of Gaunt, because

    a. he enjoys wielding power
    b. he doesn't know which one is right
    c. he's afraid of Bolingbroke
    d. *a* and *c* but not *b*
    e. *b* and *c* but not *a*

95. The term that Bolingbroke is banished is

    a. four years
    b. six years
    c. ten years

96. When the powerful John of Gaunt, uncle to Richard, dies, Richard, making a mistake,

    a. orders Gaunt to be buried anonymously
    b. banishes Gaunt's wife to Elba
    c. seizes all of Gaunt's assets

97. The Duke of York, another uncle of Richard, argues that Richard should not deny Bolingbroke's property

    a. on the grounds that Richard should respect the laws of succession since by them he was crowned king
    b. on the grounds that Bolingbroke's father was a dear old fellow and like a father to Richard
    c. on the grounds that the common people will spit at him as he passes in the street

98. The three friends of Richard, with the smarmy names, whom Bolingbroke has sworn to weed out, are

    a. _____

    b. _____

    c. _____

99. In the deposition scene, the object Richard asks for is

    a. a sword so that he can maintain a shallow dignity
    b. a mirror so that he can see what suffering has done to his face
    c. a horse so that he can ride out of there

100. The Duchess of York begs her husband

    a. to reveal the Oxford plot to Richard immediately
    b. not ever to reveal the Oxford plot
    c. to accept the fact that boys will be boys

101. The murderer of Richard is

    a. Henry IV
    b. the Duke of Aumerle
    c. Sir Pierce of Exton

Is your British history coming back to you? Surely you remember that Bolingbroke becomes Henry IV. So, move on.

1 Henry IV

102. The play begins with Henry IV yearning for a trip

    a. to the warm lands of the Mediterranean
    b. to the Holy Land
    c. to the grave of his father, John of Gaunt

103. First, Henry has to deal with the rebels in

     a. Scotland
     b. Ireland
     c. Wales
     d. *a* and *c* but not *b*
     e. *b* and *c* but not *a*
     (Do you hate this kind of question or is it fun?)

104. Hotspur, that "mad fellow of the north," angers Henry IV
     by

     a. making snide remarks about Hal, Henry's son
     b. bringing his dog to the throne room
     c. refusing to surrender his prisoners

105. Poins, Hal's friend, convinces Hal to

     a. join him on a trip to Brighton
     b. join in a robbery and joke on Falstaff
     c. go with him to the Boar's Head Tavern

106. The character in the morality plays that Falstaff is
     reminiscent of is

     a. Everyman
     b. the Pantaloon
     c. the Vice

107.   "At my nativity
           The front of heaven was full of fiery shapes,
           Of burning cressets; and at my birth
           The frame and huge foundation of the earth
           Shak'd like a coward."

The character saying this, who thinks himself so unusual, is:

    a. Hotspur
    b. Glendower
    c. Mortimer

108. "The hope and expectation of thy time
     Is ruin'd, and the soul of every man
     Prophetically do forethink thy fall."

These lines, spoken by Henry IV, describe _____.

109. Falstaff has mustered 150 soldiers by:

    a. unloading the prisons
    b. pressing revolted tapsters
    c. forcing younger sons
    d. taking "fees for substitutions"
    e. disguising women as soldiers
    f. all of the above
    g. all of the above but *e*

110. Hal and Hotspur finally meet at

    a. the battle of Shrewsbury
    b. the battle of Agincourt
    c. the battle of Bosworth Field

111. Hal is forgiven by his father because

    a. he saved his father's life
    b. he rejected Falstaff and Poins
    c. he saved his brother's life

Continue right on.

2 Henry IV

112. At the beginning of *2 Henry IV*, Northumberland receives
     word that his son Hotspur

   a. has fought Hal and won and will arrive home soon
   b. has been seriously wounded but will recover
   c. is dead

113. Falstaff's demeanor with the Lord Chief Justice is

   a. respectful
   b. arrogant
   c. fawning

114. In the tavern the Prince and Poins to fool Falstaff
     disguise themselves as

   a. tapsters
   b. pantlers
   c. ostlers

115. While the King is sleeping, Hal comes in, and, thinking
     that his father has died, he

   a. puts pennies on his eyelids
   b. takes the crown that was lying next to him
   c. kneels by the bed and sobs hysterically

116. The last advice that the dying King gives to Hal is to

   a. busy young men in foreign quarrels
   b. mentor your brother John
   c. stay out of the taverns

117. When Hal as Henry V meets the Lord Chief Justice he

    a. imprisons him because the Justice put him in prison
    b. banishes him to the Antibes
    c. says he will depend upon the Justice as a father

Now Hal, who has finished serving his apprenticeship, ascends the throne as Henry V.

Henry V

118. The insulting gift the French send to Henry that cements his desire to war against France is

    a. a crown of thorns
    b. a box of petits fours
    c. a tun of tennis balls

119. The opening of Laurence Olivier's film *Henry V* takes place

    a. in the court of Henry V
    b. backstage at the Globe during Shakespeare's day
    c. on the battlefield

120. The opening of Kenneth Branagh's *Henry V* takes place

    a. in the court of Henry V
    b. backstage at a large theater in our day
    c. on the field in France

121. The final conflict between the English and French takes place

    a. before the castle of Agincourt
    b. on the battlefield of Rouen
    c. on Bosworth Field

122. The argument Will offers about a soldier's fate is

    a. it's the soldier's fault if he dies without absolution
    b. it's the king's responsibility for the soldier's soul
    c. it's the soldier's duty to watch out for himself

123. Henry's prayer before the battle that begins "O God of battles! steel my soldiers' hearts . . ." is

    a. a plea that the soldiers will be unable to calculate the numbers against them
    b. a plea for forgiveness for the murder of Richard II
    c. a promise to accomplish more penitential service
    d. all of the above
    e. a and b but not c

124. The event that most angers Henry is

    a. the French taunting him about his soldiers and equipment
    b. the death of the Duke of York
    c. the killing of the luggage boys

125. The number of French killed, according to Shakespeare, is

    a. twenty-five hundred
    b. five thousand
    c. ten thousand

126. Henry's wooing of Katherine is difficult because

    a. she doesn't understand much of what he says
    b. she doesn't want to be a prize of the war
    c. he isn't very good at wooing

Answers

The Early Comedies: *The Comedy of Errors*

1. b. The "absurd statute," a device sometimes used by Shakespeare to initiate the plot of a comedy, is that any Syracusan born entering the bay of Ephesus will be put to death unless he can pay a ransom of a thousand marks. You must admit that's somewhat absurd.

2. c. Antipholus of Syracuse is in Ephesus because he is looking for his twin brother, whom he has not seen since they were separated at sea during a horrendous storm.

3. c. The errors of the play result from the two sets of twins, unaware of each other's existence and consequently mistaken for each other.

4. c. An important prop is a gold chain ordered by Antipholus of Ephesus from the merchant Angelo, who mistakenly hands it to Antipholus of Syracuse. Antipholus of Ephesus later requests the chain from Angelo; they argue; Angelo has Antipholus of Ephesus arrested. An additional complication is that Antipholus of Ephesus has promised it to the courtesan, and she demands it because she gave him a ring. Eventually, the chain is returned to its rightful owner. Did you follow all that?

5. f. Antipholus has had many adventures in Ephesus, including dining with a woman he's never seen before (a), being given a gold chain that he didn't order (b), and then being charged with denying possession of it (d). But he has not been arrested as a Syracusan.

6. e. Dromio of Syracuse also has had many adventures in Ephesus. He's been beaten by his master (a), hotly pursued by the kitchen wench (b), and provided money for his master to get out of jail (d), but he doesn't consider his master mad, since strange things have happened to him too.

7. b. The Broadway musical was called *The Boys from Syracuse*. It ran for 235 performances in 1938.

8. 1. c. Luciana (II. i.7).

2. e. Antipholus of Syracuse (II.ii.30).

3. d. Balthasar (III.i.26).

4. a. Dromio of Syracuse (IV.ii.58).

5. b. Dromio of Ephesus (IV.iv.30).

6. f. Abbess (V.i.70–71).

The Taming of the Shrew

9. c. Sly is being thrown out of the alehouse by the hostess because he will not or cannot pay for the glasses he has broken. The hostess goes to seek the constable; Sly falls into a drunken sleep.

10. b. A lord, returning from the hunt, comes across Sly. As a jest, the lord dresses Sly in fine clothes and places him in a wealthy environment to persuade Sly that he is a lord in reality.

11. b. Petruchio comes from Verona "to wive it wealthily in Padua" (I.ii.75).

12. c. Lorenzo is not a suitor of Bianca. He is not even in the play. If you thought he was, you're probably thinking of Lucentio.

13. a. Lucentio disguises himself as Tranio, and Gremio presents him to Baptista as Cambio, "cunning in Greek, Latin and other languages" (II.i. 82).

14. c. Petruchio is dressed in "a new hat and an old jerkin, a pair of old breeches thrice turned, a pair of boots that have been candle-cases, one buckled, another laced, an old rusty sword ta'en out of the town armoury"(III.ii.42–45).

15. b. Petruchio says, "Katherine, that cap of yours becomes you not;/Off with that bauble, throw it under foot" (V.ii.120–21), which she evidently does, thus proving herself the most obedient of the women of the party.

16. "I am ashamed that women are so *simple*,
    To offer war where they should *kneel* for peace"

(V.ii.161–62)

17. a. *Kiss Me Kate* is the title of the 1948 musical. It starred Alfred Drake and Patricia Morison. The 1953 film starred Howard Keel and Kathryn Grayson. A Broadway revival in 1999 featured Brian Stokes Mitchell and Marin Mazzie in the major roles.

18. Elizabeth Taylor played Katherine and Richard Burton Petruchio in the 1967 film.

The Two Gentlemen of Verona

19. c. Valentine is going to Milan to the Duke's court.

20. b. He is going to acquire honor, because he can't seem to find any at home.

21. c. Don Antonio, Proteus's father, speaks these lines, to justify sending Proteus to Milan too (I.iii.20–21).

22. a. Proteus begins to woo Sylvia, the girl Valentine loves.

23. b. Sylvia is not too happy with Proteus's courtship, but she does give him a picture of herself.

24. c. Launce's dog is named Crab.

25. c. The rope ladder is the device by which Valentine hopes to rescue Sylvia, so that they can steal off to be married. Proteus, however, reveals the plan to the Duke, the plan is thwarted, and Valentine banished (III.i.).

26. a. Julia disguises herself as Sebastian, the first of Shakespeare's "breeches" parts, and is employed as a page by Proteus (IV.ii.).

27 a. The part of Launce in Shakespeare's company would have been played by Will Kempe.

28. b. The rock musical *The Two Gentlemen of Verona* was performed in the 1970s.

Love's Labor's Lost

29. c. That was too easy. The initial *l* in each word of the title identifies alliteration.

30. c. The setting of the play is in the park of Ferdinand, King of Navarre, a region in northwest Spain. Thanks to Ernest Hemingway and his novel *The Sun Also Rises,* it is famed for the running of the bulls in Pamplona, its capital and major city.

31. c. The King , Longaville, Dumayne, and a very reluctant Berowne vow to live and study together for three years, to eschew the company of women, and to eat and sleep sparingly.

32. a. Ironically, the first to break the vow is the King.

33. d. Berowne is the last.

34. a. Holofernes is a pedant, and his character is a caricature of the English schoolmaster.

35. a. The young men disguise themselves as Muscovites, which does not fool the women for a minute.

36. c. Rosaline is compelled to return home because she receives the distressing news of the death of her father, which turns the tone of the play from frivolity to solemnity.

37. a. Rosaline tells Berowne that he must spend a year visiting the sick and using all "the fierce endeavour of your wit" to make those in pain smile (V.ii.863).

38. c. In 2000, Kenneth Branagh produced and starred in a musical version of the play, updated to the 1930s.

The Early History Plays: *Richard III*

39. a. True. The red rose is the symbol of the House of Lancaster, the white rose the House of York.
   b. True. Richard is a Yorkist.

40. a. Richard's opening soliloquy is an example of irony. The words suggest that all is peaceful and harmonious in the House of York; but Richard's attitude is quite opposite.

41. c. Richard does have a crooked back and a withered hand, but he does not have a glass eye (at least Shakespeare didn't give him one).

42. c. Clarence has been arrested and is on his way to the Tower.

43. c. Richard gives Anne a ring (I.ii).

44. c. Margaret curses everyone except Buckingham. Instead, she kisses his hand "in sign of league and amity" with him (I.iii.281) and warns him to "take heed of yonder dog" (I.iii.289).

45. a. Buckingham balks at the idea of killing the little princes. His reluctance annoys Richard, who remarks, "High reaching Buckingham grows circumspect" (IV.ii.31).

46. c. Dighton and Forrest are the murderers of the little princes. Tyrrel says that though they were "flesh'd villains" and "bloody dogs," they "wept like to children in their deaths' sad story" (IV.iii.8).

47. a. Because Richard fears Stanley will join with Richmond, he insists that Stanley leave his son George behind (IV.iv.495).

48. The first ghost who appears to torture Richard in his dreams is Buckingham (V.iii.167–68).

49. a. The last battle, in which Richard is slain, is fought on Bosworth Field.

50. c. Richmond, of the House of Lancaster, takes over at the end of the play.

Actors of *Richard III*

51. a. Richard Burbage (1567–1619) was the actor who created most of Shakespeare's leading roles, including Richard III. Three years younger than Shakespeare, he and Shakespeare were colleagues for twenty years, first at the Theatre and then at the Globe.

52. b. Colley Cibber (1635–1710) rewrote *Richard III,* explaining in his autobiography, "I brought *Richard the Third* to the stage with such alterations as I thought not improper." Since the Master of the Revels insisted on omitting most of the first act, including Margaret's curse and Clarence's dream, Cibber added speeches from the other *Henrys,* and two scenes of his own invention.

53. d. David Garrick (1717–79) was as successful in *Richard III* as he was in *Hamlet.* He so intimidated Mrs. Siddons onstage, that she forgot his instructions to follow him step by step (so that he could keep his face to the audience) and was reminded of them only after an even more ferocious look from him.

54. e. Charles Kean (1811–68) never equaled his father as an actor. Nevertheless, his Richard III drew great crowds at Covent Garden. He also was a scholar, and his research for his lavish productions was meticulous.

55. f. Edmund Kean (1787–1830) experienced both extravagant success and painful humiliation with Richard. His debut at Drury Lane was highly praised, but a year later when he refused to play Richard in Boston, he antagonized American audiences and was forced to end his tour prematurely.

56. g. Richard Mansfield (1854–1907) wanted to stress the progress of Richard from youth to age; he thus dated all the events in the program. He used some of Cibber's alterations but added some innovations of his own, particularly in the scene with Anne and in the scene with the clergymen.

57. i. Laurence Olivier (1907–89) emphasized the wily, witty quality of Richard in his film performance, which was complemented by his elaborate makeup.

58. c. Richard Dreyfuss (1947–) struggles to play a gay Richard in *The Goodbye Girl* (1977), a film that earned him an Oscar for Best Actor.

59. h. Ian McKellen (1939–) collaborates with the film viewer in his (1995) interpretation of Richard, sharing his plans and jokes as well as his murderous intents with the viewing audience.

60. j. Al Pacino (1940–) filmed his Richard on the streets of New York and in *Looking for Richard* (1996) makes the play accessible to all kinds of audiences.

More answers. Are you getting them right?

Titus Andronicus

61. d. Titus, returning victorious from the war with the Goths, says that he has contributed "five and twenty valiant sons,/ Half the number that King Priam had" (I.i.79–80).

62. c. The eldest son of the Queen of the Goths is chosen to appease the spirits of Titus's dead sons. The Roman rites of sacrificing the loser's representative require that he have his limbs hewed and burned in a sacrificial fire.

63. b. The new emperor, Saturninus, is angered when Lavinia rejects him in favor of Bassianus.

64. a. At the hand of his father, Titus, who says, "What, vil-

lain boy!/Barr'st me my way to Rome?" (I.i.290–91), as he stabs Mutius.

65. a. Aaron persuasively suggests that the boys cease their quarreling, and since the woods are "ruthless, dreadful, deaf, and dull," there they can take their turns and serve their lust (II.i.128–30).

66. g. During the hunt, Lavinia is raped (a); Bassianus is murdered (b); Lavinia's hands are severed (c); and her tongue is cut out (d). She does not find or lose Aaron's bag of gold (e).

67. c. Upon viewing Lavinia's mutilation, Marcus compares her to Philomel, in Ovid's *Metamorphoses,* raped by her brother-in-law Tereus, who cut out her tongue so that she would not reveal his villainy.

68. d. Bassianus is murdered for all the reasons stated: he married Lavinia, when the emperor desired her (a); he came across Tamora and Aaron making love in the woods (b); and he fit Tamora's plan for avenging her son's death (c).

69. a. Tamora plans to implicate Titus's sons in Bassianus's murder with a planted letter.

70. c. In order to save his sons, who have been falsely accused of murdering the emperor's brother, Titus, Marcus, or Lucius can send the emperor his chopped-off hand, and "he for the same/Will send thee hither both thy sons alive" (III.i.154–55). This is, of course, a false promise

71. a. Titus says, "If there were reason for these miseries,/ Then into limits could I bind my woes" (III.i.220–21). He recognizes that the woes he experiences go beyond reason.

72. e. All of these grotesqueries are to be carried out in Titus's effort to avenge the deaths of his children. Lavinia carries Titus's hand in her teeth (a); Titus takes one head of the sons (b); Marcus takes the head of another (b); Lucius vows to

raise an army and return to "make proud Saturnine and his empress/Beg at the gates, like Tarquin and his queen" (d) (III.i.298–99).

73. d. Lavinia identifies her attackers by writing their names in the sand with a stick held in her mouth.

74. c. Tamora's liaison with Aaron becomes evident with the birth of her black baby, which the nurse describes as "A joyless, dismal, black, and sorrowful issue . . . as loathsome as a toad" (IV.ii.66–67).

75. e. Titus accomplishes all of the listed gross activities.

76. g. At the final banquet, Lavinia is killed by her father, because her shame was too great (a); Tamora is also killed by Titus after eating the flesh of her sons (b); Saturninus kills Titus (c), and he in turn is killed by Lucius (d). The others are not present: Demetrius and Chiron have metamorphosed into a pie, and the black baby has been sent to the Goths (V.iii).

The Histories

77. a. The Chorus (*Henry V*, Prologue. 1–4) laments the limitations of the stage and urges the audience to use their imaginations.

78. c. In this soliloquy, Prince Hal (*1 Henry IV*, I.ii.218–19) reveals that he is playing the role of the profligate, biding his time before revealing his true character.

79. i. Lady Percy (*1 Henry IV*, II.iii 99–101) teases her husband, Hotspur, who is leaving without telling her his destination.

80 j. Lord Mowbray (*Richard II*, I.iii.159–62) has been exiled forever from England by Richard II, and he grieves at this sentence.

81. h. The elderly Justice Shallow (*2 Henry IV*, III.ii.48–50)

remembers the skill of his dead friend with the bow and tries to accept his death.

82. k. King Richard (*Richard II*, V.v.1–5), is in prison and, realizing he will probably not survive, struggles to understand his situation.

83. f. Hotspur (*1 Henry IV*, I.iii.201–7) heatedly urges an effort to claim honor.

84. g. John of Gaunt (*Richard II*, II.1.61–66) with his dying breath strives to convince Richard II to mend his negligent behavior.

85. d. King Henry IV (*2 Henry IV*, III.i.5–8), ill and guilt-ridden, is unable to sleep.

86. n. The Duke of York (*Richard II*, II.iii.86–89) scolds his nephew Bolingbroke who has dared to return from exile before his time.

87. l. Warwick (*2 Henry IV*, III.1.80–85) tells King Henry that he should not be surprised that Richard's prophecy of division among the lords was coming true.

88. e. Henry V (*Henry V*, III.i.1–7) urges his troops onward in the siege of Harfleur.

89. m. The common soldier Will (*Henry V*, IV.i.147–51) considers the plight of the men the night before the battle of Agincourt.

90. d. Henry IV (*2 Henry IV*, IV.v. 134–38) laments that at his death the riotous Prince Hal will take over.

91. b. Before the battle of Shrewsbury, Falstaff (*1 Henry IV*, V.i.137–42) questions the ideal of honour and concludes that it is worthless.

Richard II

92. c. Richard II is the only son of Edward, the Black Prince, who was the eldest son of Edward III, and died in Spain at the age of forty-six.

93. f. Richard's flaws include all mentioned except religiosity.

94. d. Richard stops the contest between Bolingbroke and Mowbray not because he doesn't know which is right, but because he's a little nervous about Bolingbroke and his father, Gaunt, and because he enjoys the trappings of power.

95. b. Richard first banishes Bolingbroke for ten years but, upon seeing Gaunt's grief at the sentence, shortens the term by four years: "Six frozen winters spent, / Return with welcome home from banishment" (I.iii.211–12).

96. c. At Gaunt's death, Richard seizes all of Gaunt's property, which now belongs to Bolingbroke, to use in his Irish wars (II.i.160–61).

97. a. The Duke of York argues that Richard came to the throne by the laws of succession, and thus should respect the heritage of others; if he does not do so, he "pluck[s] a thousand dangers" on his head (II.i.205).

98. Bushy (a), Bagot (b), and Green (c) evoke images of maggots in bushy gardens.

99. b. In the deposition scene, Richard calls for a mirror, "That it may show me what a face I have, / Since it is bankrout of his majesty" (IV.i.266–67).

100. b. The Duchess of York tries desperately to keep her husband from revealing the plot of the Oxford men against the life of the king.

101. c. Sir Pierce of Exton murders Richard II; Henry IV says, "Though I did wish him dead, / I hate the murderer" (V.vi.39–40).

1 Henry IV

102. b. At the beginning of the play, Henry speaks longingly of the trip he has vowed to the Holy Land.

103. d. News arrives of rebellions in Wales where Mortimer was taken by Glendower and in the North where Hotspur fought with Douglas.

104. c. Hotspur refuses to surrender the prisoners he captured in Scotland, and Henry says, "Send us your prisoners, or you will hear of it" (I.iii.124).

105. b. Poins convinces Hal to watch the robbery Falstaff and Gadshill commit, and then to rob the robbers.

106. c. The character of the morality plays that Falstaff is sometimes likened to is the Vice.

107. b. The speaker about his unusual birth is the superstitious Glendower (III.i.12–16).

108. In this speech expressing his evaluation of his son, Hal, Henry IV worries about the future of the country (III.ii.36–39).

109. g. Falstaff admits that he has "misused the king's press damnably," that he has emptied the prisons, taken "unjust servingmen," "revolted tapsters," "younger sons to younger brothers" and allowed those who could to buy off their service (IV.ii.12–52). The only means he has not used to muster troops is to disguise women as men.

110. a. Hal and Hotspur finally meet at the battle of Shrewsbury.

111. a. The King forgives Hal on the battlefield after Hal fends off the Earl of Douglas. Henry says, "Thou has redeem'd thy lost opinion, / And show'd thou mak'st some tender of my life" (V.iv.48–49).

2 *Henry IV*

112. c. Northumberland receives word that his son Hotspur is dead (I.i.112).

113. b. Falstaff is arrogant with the Lord Chief Justice (I.ii).

114. a. In the tavern scene, the Prince and Poins disguise themselves as tapsters and overhear Falstaff's description of them (II.iv.). (Tapsters are the equivalent of today's busboys or waiters; pantlers are stewards or butlers; hostlers are those who care for horses.)

115. b. Believing his father has died, Hal picks up the crown from the pillow, puts it on, and leaves the room (IV.v).

116. a. Because he feels the crown is not secure, Henry urges Hal to busy the young men "with foreign quarrels" (IV.v.215).

117. c. The new Henry V tells the Lord Chief Justice, "You shall be as a father to my youth" (V.ii.117).

Henry V

118. c. The Dauphin of France sends Henry V a cask of tennis balls.

119. b. The opening of Olivier's film takes place backstage at the Globe, during Shakespeare's day, with Henry V anxiously awaiting his cue from the Archbishops.

120. b. The opening of Kenneth Branagh's *Henry V* is set backstage in a contemporary theater with the Chorus in modern dress.

121. a. The final conflict takes place before the castle of Agincourt.

122. b. Will says, "If these men do not die well, it will be a black matter for the king that led them to it" (IV.i.151–52).

123. d. Henry prays first that the soldiers will not be able to calculate the numbers opposing them; then he prays that the Lord will not think about the murder of Richard II on this particular day; and finally he promises that he will do even more in penance for his father's fault (IV.i.306–22).

124. c. Henry is most angry when he hears of the killing of the boys, and then orders every soldier to kill his prisoners (IV.vii.10–11).

125. c. According to Shakespeare, there are ten thousand French killed in the battle, while the English lost three nobles and five and twenty others (IV.viii.92).

126. a. The courtship of Henry and Katherine is difficult because his French is rudimentary and she knows only the names of a few body parts in English.

ACT III

Professionals

Now that you've successfully passed the amateur and apprentice stages, you've become a Professional. Professionals, like actors and playwrights, are not necessarily superstars. They do not know everything. They're journeymen, they "swell the scene," they've learned a trade or an art but are yet not masters of it. In our time they are student teachers, community theater directors and actors, college students, retirees who've taken a course or two at the local adult learning center just for fun, perhaps even an engineer or computer geek who functions "outside the box." They have traveled to distant sites to see a specific play; they have seen *Hamlet* onstage at least ten times. They've seen the plays made into film adaptations as they've been released, including some of the more controversial contemporary ones.

Shakespeare, too, is no longer an apprentice. Still exploring character and behavior, he has not yet reached or become a major player. Like a journeyman, he is a "sharer" in the company and makes a daily wage, but his major plays are still ahead of him.

In this section you'll find quizzes for three mature comedies, *The Merchant of Venice*, *Much Ado About Nothing*, and *Twelfth Night;* and three problem plays, *All's Well that Ends*

Well, Measure for Measure, and *Troilus and Cressida.* Framing each section, for a change of pace, are three entr'actes: Motifs, Dreams, and Music.

There are 110 questions for you Professionals. Answers begin on page 103; each, as usual, is worth one point. Half or more correct answers moves you on to the Major Players!

Remember:

Just make the score,

And then you'll catch the fever to do more!

Motifs

In many of his plays, Shakespeare links words, images, phrases, and actions into a motif, a recurring thematic element, that supports the major idea, and creates a cultural background and/or adds atmosphere.

To test your professional skills, match the play below with the motif that occurs most frequently.

Play

1. *Othello*
2. *Hamlet*
3. *2 Henry IV*
4. *King Lear*
5. *Macbeth*
6. *The Merchant of Venice*
7. *Much Ado About Nothing*
8. *Richard II*
9. *Romeo and Juliet*
10. *Twelfth Night*

Motif

a. a flash of light
b. an unweeded garden
c. drowning
d. animality
e. questioning
f. hazard and risk
g. eavesdropping
h. disease and physical failure
i. blood
j. sight and awareness

The first of the three skillful comedies is . . .

The Merchant of Venice

11. One of the major themes of the play is

    a. nature vs. fortune
    b. merit vs. nature
    c. justice vs. mercy

12. At the opening of the play, the merchant Antonio says that he is

    a. questioning his single state, and sad that he turns girls off
    b. weary and sad, but can't explain why
    c. worried about his fortunes tossing on the sea

13. The reason Bassanio needs funds from Antonio to woo Portia is that

    a. he's already spent an earlier loan from Antonio
    b. he wants to outfit an elegant ship to travel to Belmont and make a dramatic arrival
    c. his father has cut off his allowance because he's such a spendthrift

14. Portia's distant suitors include all but one of the following:

    a. the Neapolitan Prince
    b. Don Pedro of Tuscany
    c. the County Palatine
    d. Monsieur LeBon
    e. Baron Falconbridge

15. An important reason that the Christians scorn Shylock is that

    a. he won't eat pork
    b. he wears a yarmulke
    c. he is a usurer

16. The three suitors who appear to woo Portia are (you're cheating if you look above)

    a. Bassanio   b. _____   c. _____

17. One character omitted from Olivier's film of *The Merchant of Venice* is

    a. Launcelot Gobbo
    b. Solanio
    c. Tubal

18. The song "Tell me, where is fancy bred?" is a clue to the correct casket because

    a. it rhymes with *wed*, thus suggesting a future with Portia
    b. it rhymes with *bed*, which would be the ultimate goal of the courtship with Portia
    c. it rhymes with *lead*, which is the correct choice
    d. all of the above

19. The engagement of Portia's maid, Nerissa, to Gratiano depends upon

    a. Bassanio's winning Portia
    b. Lorenzo's winning Jessica
    c. Portia's winning the case for Antonio

20. Portia's nom de plume when she travels to Venice is

    a. Bellario
    b. Balthasar
    c. Cesario

21. In Olivier's film, Shylock's exit after the trial is memorable
    because

    a. he emits an elongated howl
    b. he crawls out of the room
    c. the young lords lift and shove him from the room

22. After the trial, Portia rejects Bassanio's offer of three
    thousand ducats; instead she requests

    a. Antonio's gloves and Bassanio's ring
    b. Antonio's handkerchief and Bassanio's ring
    c. Antonio's scarf and Bassanio's ring

Another of Shakespeare's mature comedies, which received
a colorful film production by Kenneth Branagh in 1993 is . . .

Much Ado About Nothing

23. The title, *Much Ado About Nothing,* suggests

    a. a pun on "noting"
    b. a revelry to no purpose
    c. a silly mistake

24. In the opening of Kenneth Branagh's film, Emma
    Thompson (Beatrice) is

    a. knitting a sweater for her soldier brother
    b. sipping lemonade
    c. reading aloud one of the songs from the play

25. In this film, the role of Don Pedro's bastard brother is played by

    a. Denzel Washington
    b. Keanu Reeves
    c. Mel Gibson

26. Don John's accomplices in villainy are

    a. Oliver and Orlando
    b. Dogberry and Verges
    c. Conrade and Borachio

27. In the ball scene, the Prince wooes Hero for

    a. himself
    b. Claudio
    c. Don John

28. Claudio is gulled into believing Hero is unfaithful by

    a. a sight trick
    b. a bed trick
    c. a hearing trick

29. The deed that Beatrice requires of Benedick before she will accept his love is

    a. to leave the service
    b. to shave his beard
    c. to kill Claudio

30. Claudio's penance for slandering Hero is to

    a. go into exile in Mantua
    b. hang an epitaph upon her tomb
    c. serve 30 days in jail

31. One of the themes of the play might be expressed as

    a. true love develops through time, trial, and trust
    b. true love develops through sight, sacrifice, and sense
    c. true love develops through dining, dancing, and
       drinking

32.–36. Select the character described by the following pas-
        sages:

    a. Beatrice   b. Benedick   e. Verges
    c. Claudio   d. Hero

32. "He hath borne himself beyond the promise of his age,
    doing, in the figure of a lamb, the feats of a lion; he had
    indeed better bettered expectation."

    _____

33. "Give not this rotten orange to your friend:
    She's but the sign and semblance of her honour.
    Behold how like a maid she blushes here!
    O, what authority and show of truth
    Can cunning sin cover itself withal!"

    _____

34. "A good old man, sir; he will be talking; as they say, when
    the age is in the wit is out."

    _____

35. "She speaks poniards, and every word stabs: if her breath
    were as terrible as her terminations, there were no living
    near her; she would infect to the north pole . . . I would
    not marry her if she were endowed with all that Adam had
    left him before he transgressed: she would have made

Hercules have turned spit, yea, and have cleft his club to make the fire too."

36. "From the crown of his head to the sole of his foot, he is all mirth: he hath twice or thrice cut Cupid's bow-string and the little hangman dare not shoot at him; he hath a heart as sound as a bell and his tongue is the clapper, for what his heart thinks his tongue speaks."

Another favorite comedy of Shakespeare's professional years is . . .

Twelfth Night

37. The title, *Twelfth Night,* refers to

   a. the twelfth night after Shakespeare was knighted by Queen Elizabeth
   b. the twelfth knight of King Arthur's court
   c. the Feast of the Epiphany, twelve days after Christmas on the Christian calendar

38. In the first act of *Twelfth Night,* Olivia is mourning for

   a. her father
   b. her brother
   c. her first lover, who left her suddenly after their long engagement

39. The name Viola assumes in her disguise is

   a. Cesario
   b. Ganymede
   c. Sebastian

40. Sir Toby Belch is Olivia's

    a. guardian, since her father died
    b. cousin once removed
    c. uncle

41. One of the following is *not* enamored of Olivia:

    a. Orsino   b. Malvolio
    c. Sebastian   d. Sir Andrew Aguecheek
    e. Antonio

42. One of the statements of the play is that

    a. too much carousing brings its own punishment
    b. one should enjoy life while young
    c. one should mourn family members seriously

43.–47. Sort out the couples at the end of the play. Two characters are losers. So who ends with whom?

    a. Sir Andrew Aguecheek   e. Olivia
    b. Sir Toby Belch   f. Orsino
    c. Malvolio   g. Sebastian
    d. Maria   h. Viola

43. _____

44. _____

45. _____

46. _____

Identify the character described in the following speeches: Possible characters:

    a. Sir Andrew Aguecheek   d. Malvolio
    b. Sir Toby Belch   e. Olivia
    c. Feste   f. Viola

47. "He plays o' the viol-de -gamboys, and speaks three or four languages word for word without book, and hath all the good gifts of nature."

_____

48. "Not yet old enough for a man, nor young enough for a boy; as a squash is before 'tis a peascod . . . He is very well-favoured and he speaks very shrewishly; one would think his mother's milk were scarce out of him."

_____

49. "The devil a puritan that he is, or any thing constantly, but a time-pleaser; an affectioned ass, that cons state without book and utters it by good swarths: the best persuaded of himself, so crammed, as he thinks, with excellencies, that it is his grounds of faith that all that look on him love him."

_____

50. "This fellow is wise enough to play the fool;
And to do that well craves a kind of wit:
He must observe their mood on whom he jests,
The quality of persons, and the time . . .
                         This is a practice
As full of labour as a wise man's art."

_____

51.   "The element itself, till seven years' heat,
Shall not behold her face at ample view;
But, like a cloistress, she will veiled walk
And water once a day her chamber round
With eye-offending brine."

_____

Here's one of those entr'actes I promised.

Dreams

Characters' dreams in Shakespeare are usually nightmares. But some are prophetic, and a few are pleasant wish-fulfillment fantasies. Still, they all attest to Shakespeare's intuitive understanding of the unconscious.

Here are the dreamers and, to help you out, the titles of the plays they are in.

a. Antigonus, *The Winter's Tale*
b. Bottom, *Midsummer Night's Dream*
c. Caliban, *The Tempest*
d. George, Duke of Clarence, *Richard III*
e. Cleopatra, *Antony and Cleopatra*
f. The Doctor, *Macbeth*
g. Hamlet, *Hamlet*
h. Hermia, *Midsummer Night's Dream*
i. Julius Caesar, *Julius Caesar*
j. King Henry V, *Henry V*
k. Mercutio, *Romeo and Juliet*
l. Richard III, *Richard III*

Match the speeches below with their speakers

52. "Give me another horse! bind up my wounds.
Have mercy, Jesu!—Soft, I did but dream.
O coward conscience how dost thou afflict me!"

_____

53. "Ay, me, for pity! what a dream was here!
Lysander, look how I do quake with fear:
Methought a serpent eat my heart away,
And you sat smiling at his cruel prey."

_____

54.   "True, I talk of dreams,
    Which are the children of an idle brain,
    Begot of nothing but vain fantasy,
    Which is as thin of substance as the air
    And more inconstant than the wind."

    _____

55. "I dream'd there was an Emperor Antony:
    O, such another sleep, that I might see
    But such another man!"

    _____

56. "How ill white hairs become a fool and jester!
    I have long dream'd of such a kind of man,
    So surfeit-swell'd, so old and so profane;
    But, being awak'd, I do despise my dream."

    _____

57. "O, I have pass'd a miserable night,
    So full of fearful dreams, of ugly sights,
    That, as I am a Christian faithful man,
    I would not spend another such a night,
    Though 'twere to buy a world of happy days."

    _____

58. "I have had a most rare vision. I have had a dream, past
    the wit of man to say what dream it was: man is but an ass,
    if he go about to expound this dream."

    _____

59. "She dreamt tonight she saw my statue
    Which, like a fountain with an hundred spouts,
    Did run pure blood; and many lusty Romans
    Came smiling and did bathe their hands in it."

    _____

60.　　　　　"And then, in dreaming,
　　The clouds methought would open and show riches
　　Ready to drop upon me, that, when I wak'd,
　　I cried to dream again."

_____

61. "O God, I could be bounded in a nutshell and count myself
　　a king of infinite space, were it not that I have bad
　　dreams."

_____

62. "I have heard, but not believ'd, the spirits o'th'dead
　　May walk again: if such thing be, thy mother
　　Appear'd to me last night, for ne'er was dream so
　　Like a waking. To me comes a creature,
　　Sometimes her head on one side, some another;
　　I ne'er saw a vessel of like sorrow,
　　So fill'd and so becoming."

_____

63.　　　　　"Unnatural deeds
　　Do breed unnatural troubles: infected minds
　　To their deaf pillows will discharge their secrets:
　　More needs she the divine than the physician."

_____

Problem Plays

The next three quizzes deal with works that don't fit comfortably into any category. They're darker than comedies and lighter than tragedies. So what is Shakespeare doing? Maybe he's concentrating upon his major tragedies, which he's also writing about this time. But Professionals shouldn't have any problem with these questions. Right?

All's Well That Ends Well

64. In the first scene, the Countess, Bertram, and Helena are
in mourning for

    a. Bertram's father
    b. Helena's mother
    c. the Countess's sister

65. The character Shakespeare creates in Bertram is

    a. a studious young man
    b. an immature and selfish young man
    c. a brave young warrior

66. "I know him a notorious liar,
    Think him a great way fool, solely a coward."

    This speech describes

    a. Bertram
    b. Lafeu
    c. Parolles

67. The deed that Helena performs for the King is

    a. to teach him Latin
    b. to cure him of his disease
    c. to bring him a lovely young maiden

68. The sentence that best illustrates the theme of this play is

    a. heaven helps those who help themselves
    b. necessity is the mother of invention
    c. the grass is always greener on the other side of the
       fence

69. Bertram sets two "impossible" tasks for Helena to complete before he will accept her as a wife. One deals with an object, the other an action. The object is

    a. a chain
    b. a book
    c. a ring

70. The action is

    a. to claim a senate seat
    b. to beget his child
    c. to renounce her father's teaching

71. In the bed trick

    a. Diana is substituted for Helena
    b. Helena is substituted for Diana
    c. Mariana is substituted for them both

72. Parolles is trapped into vowing to recover his unit's

    a. cash box
    b. flag
    c. drum

73. True or False
    At the end of the play

    a. Bertram accepts Helena as his wife _____
    b. Diana is provided a dowry _____
    c. Parolles is banished _____

Measure for Measure

74.   "[He] scarce confesses
That his blood flows, or that his appetite
Is more to bread than water."
The above passage describes

    a. Angelo
    b. Bernardo
    c. the Duke

75. The specific restriction upon sexual activity in Vienna that
Claudio violated was one that forbade

    a. fornicating in public
    b. impregnating before marriage
    c. fornicating with first cousins

76. The most obvious theme in *Measure for Measure* is the
conflict between the two abstract ideals of

    a. public and private responsibility
    b. love and honour
    c. justice and mercy

77. Lucio is speaking to:

"I hold you as a thing ensky'd and sainted,
By your renouncement an immortal spirit,
And to be talk'd with in sincerity,
As with a saint."

    a. Sister Francisca
    b. Mariana
    c. Isabella

78. In prison, Pompey takes up the trade of

    a. hangman
    b. license plate maker
    c. blacksmith

79. Lucio, according to the cast of characters, is

    a. a fantastic
    b. a musician
    c. a merchant

80. In the bed trick

    a. Isabella is substituted for Mariana
    b. Mariana is substituted for Isabella
    c. Juliet is substituted for Mariana

81. The phrase *cucullus non facit monachum* translates as

    a. a cockerel does not make a monarch
    b. a cuckoo doesn't fancy a monk
    c. a cowl does not make a monk

82. At the end of the play, Isabel argues for a pardon for Claudio on the grounds that

    a. his intention wasn't carried out
    b. he is suffering from a sexual disease
    c. her beauty distracted him

83. True or False:
    At the end of the play

    a. Barnardine is executed _____
    b. Claudio marries Mariana _____
    c. Ragozine is executed _____
    d. Lucio is to marry a whore _____

Troilus and Cressida

84. The Prologue announces that "hither am I come / A Prologue _____ ."

    a. "arm'd"
    b. "suited"
    c. "rob'd"

85. The one not a brother of Troilus is

    a. Hector
    b. Paris
    c. Deiphobus
    d. Diomedes

86. In the first scene, Pandarus teases Troilus about his wooing of Cressida. The metaphor he uses is

    a. baking a cake
    b. sailing the ocean
    c. climbing the Pyrenees

87. When Ulysses says to the Greeks, "Degree being vizarded, / The unworthiest shows as worthy in the mask," he means:

    a. When you don a mask, the lowest appears the grandest.
    b. When authority is disguised, all men appear level.
    c. When the temperature is hidden, everyone feels the heat.

88. According to Ulysses, the person most responsible for the stagnation of the Greeks is

    a. Ajax, because he's the most powerful soldier of the Greeks, and also the laziest
    b. Patroclus, because we know what he's doing in the tent with Achilles
    c. Agamemnon, because he's the leader of the army and has not commanded the respect of the men

89. The image through which the courtship of Troilus and Cressida is made vivid is

    a. physical taste
    b. eyesight
    c. questioning

90. The event that finally brings Achilles out of his tent to fight is

    a. the challenge from Hector
    b. the tirade from Agamemnon
    c. the death of Patroclus

91.–98. Match the speaker with the speech (one speaker appears twice).

    a. Agamemnon   e. Pandarus
    b. Cassandra   f. Thersites
    c. Cressida   g. Troilus
    d. Nestor   h. Ulysses

91.   "Women are angels, wooing:
    Things done are done; joy's soul lies in the doing."

    _____

92.   "O, when degree is shak'd,
Which is the ladder to all high designs,
The enterprise is sick."

_____

93.   "Why, she is a pearl,
Whose price hath launch'd above a thousand ships."

_____

94. "Is this the generation of love? hot blood, hot thoughts,
and hot deeds? Why, they are vipers, is love a generation
of vipers?"

_____

95. "Lechery, lechery: still, wars and lechery; nothing else
holds fashion."

_____

96.   "In the reproof of chance
Lies the true proof of men."

_____

97. "What's aught, but as 'tis valued?"

_____

98. "Cry, Troyans, cry! lend me ten thousand eyes,
And I will fill them with prophetic tears."

_____

99. "He that is proud eats up himself: pride is his own
glass, his own trumpet, his own chronicle; and whatever
praises itself but in the deed, devours the deed in the
praise."

_____

100. True or False:
     At the end of the play

     a. Cressida is dead _____
     b. Hector is dead _____
     c. Troilus is dead _____

Music

In production, directors often underscore parts of the text with music. Shakespeare too saw the benefits and influence that music might have.

Consider the passages below, then identify, if you can, the play and the speaker. The plays included are *The Two Gentlemen of Verona, Romeo and Juliet, The Merchant of Venice, Twelfth Night, Richard II*, and *Measure for Measure. Cymbeline, Antony and Cleopatra*, and *The Tempest* complete the list. Good luck.

101. "For Orpheus' lute was strung with poets' sinews,
     Whose golden touch could soften steel and stones,
     Make tigers tame and huge leviathans
     Forsake unsounded deeps to dance on sands."

     _____   _____

102.   "Music do I hear?
     Ha, ha! keep time: how sour sweet music is,
     When time is broke and no proportion kept!
     So is it in the music of men's lives."

     _____   _____

103. "I cry you mercy; you are the singer: I will say for you. It
     is 'music with her silver sound,' because musicians have
     no gold for sounding:
           'Then music with her silver sound
           With speedy help doth lend redress.' "

     _____   _____

104. "The man that hath no music in himself,
Nor is not mov'd with concord of sweet sounds,
Is fit for treasons, stratagems and spoils,
The motions of his spirit are dull as night
And his affections dark as Erebus,
Let no such man be trusted."

_____   _____

105. "If music be the food of love, play on;
Give me excess of it, that, surfeiting,
The appetite may sicken, and so die.
That strain again! It had a dying fall:
O, it came o'er my ear like the sweet sound,
That breathes upon a bank of violets,
Stealing and giving odour!"

_____   _____

106.   "Music oft hath such a charm
To make bad good, and good provoke to harm."

_____   _____

107. "Give me some music; music, moody food
Of us that trade in love."

_____   _____

108. "If this penetrate, I will consider your music the better. If
it do not, it is a vice in her ears, which horse-hairs and
calves'-guts, nor the voice of unpaved eunuch to boot, can
never amend."

_____   _____

109. "Where should this music be? I' th' air or th' earth?
It sounds no more; and, sure, it waits upon
Some god o' th' island. Sitting on a bank,

Weeping again the king my father's wrack,
This music crept by me upon the waters,
Allaying both their fury and my passion
With its sweet air."

_____   _____

And one more, from the same play as above, but by a different character:

110. "Be not afeard; the isle is full of noises,
Sounds and sweet airs, that give delight and hurt not.
Sometimes a thousand twangling instruments
Will hum about mine ears, and sometime voices
That, if I then had wak'd after long sleep,
Will make me sleep again; and then, in dreaming,
The clouds methought would open and show riches
Ready to drop upon me, that, when I wak'd,
I cried to dream again."

_____   _____

Answers

Motifs

1. d. *Othello* is filled with references to animals and animal behavior, beginning with Iago's description of Othello and Desdemona making "the beast with two backs" and "the black ram tupping your white ewe." These ugly images contribute to Iago's cynical idea of the grossness of humanity, particularly in matters of love and marriage. Later Othello picks up the same kind of imagery and speaks of toads breeding in a cistern, goats and monkeys, the tears of a crocodile.

2. e. In *Hamlet* there are over four hundred questions, beginning with the first line of the play, "Who's there?" and in-

cluding the most famous question of all, "To be or not to be, that is the question." Thus the motif is carried through literally with actual questions, but also metaphorically as Hamlet struggles to resolve the major question of avenging his father's murder.

3. h. *2 Henry IV* contains many references to illness and physical decline. Henry IV himself is ill and dies; Northumberland has been "crafty sick" while his son Hotspur has challenged the King and lost; Prince Hal is "weary"; Justices Shallow and Silence are tottering at the edge of the grave. These images reinforce the theme of England itself as corrupt and in a decline.

4. j. In *King Lear* sight is coupled with awareness. "See better, Lear," counsels Kent when Lear disowns his daughter Cordelia. Gloucester admits, after his eyes have been destroyed, that he sees better in blindness than before. In their sighted state both Lear and Gloucester misjudged their children; awareness results from physical blindness for one and from mental blindness for the other.

5. i. *Macbeth* is awash in blood. It appears in the first scene with the description of Macbeth's bravery in battle and continues oozing out of slaughtered bodies and murder after murder throughout the play. It indelibly stains the hands of Macbeth and Lady Macbeth and metaphorically signifies their brutality, ambition, and guilt.

6. f. Hazard and risk as options of behavior are explored in *The Merchant of Venice*. Antonio hazards his ships upon the sea to provide Bassanio with funds for the courtship of Portia, and thereafter the three suitors hazard their persons in Lorenzo's eloping with Jessica, Bassanio's choice of the three caskets, and Gratiano's courtship of Nerissa. There are also Shylock's wager of the three thousand ducats against Antonio's pound of flesh and Portia's venture into the court of Venice. Every char-

acter in the play takes a chance; Shylock is the only one who loses.

7. g. *Eavesdropping* is a perfect word to describe the activity of overhearing secret conversations by parties all too eager to believe what they hear, or think they hear. In *Much Ado About Nothing* Conrad thinks he overhears the Prince saying he will woo Hero for himself; both Beatrice and Benedick eavesdrop on conversations deliberately designed to gull them; Claudio overhears a conversation between Margaret and Conrad deliberately designed to gull him; and Dogberry overhears the plot to discredit Hero. The eavesdropping motif supports the idea that people hear what they want to hear and that reality resides in actions not in words.

8. b. In *Richard II,* as in all the histories, England is seen as a walled garden, with the king as gardener. In this play, however, the theme is thoroughly displayed: John of Gaunt's great speech describes England as an earthly paradise, a true Eden that has been leased out by Richard and his cronies. The theme is further developed in the Gardener's scene, in which the Gardener calls England an unweeded garden, full of pests, growing without care, and speaks sadly about those who have done no pruning.

9. a. The courtship of Romeo and Juliet is described as "too rash, too sudden, too ill-advised, too like the lightning" and, indeed, images of lightning, flashes of light, stars, and starlight permeate the play. The motif reinforces the idea of the impulsiveness and youth of the lovers.

10. c. The motif of drowning occurs in *Twelfth Night* in several ways. First, there is the literal supposed drowning of Sebastian, and the near drowning of Viola. But there is also the figurative drowning that invades the play: Olivia is drowning in grief for her brother; Malvolio is drowning in self-love; Orsino is drowning in desire for Olivia; and Toby is drowning in

liquor. Shakespeare seems to be poking fun at all his characters and suggesting that they get a grip on reality.

The Merchant of Venice

11. c. Justice and mercy comprise major thematic material. Shylock stands for justice, Portia for mercy. But Shylock's justice is more than he sought, and Portia's mercy is not without cruelty, as she makes no effort to soften the Judge's confiscation of Shylock's fortune.

12. b. At the opening of the play, Antonio says, "In sooth, I know not why I am so sad:/It wearies me . . . But how I caught it, found it, or came by it . . . I am to learn"(I.i.1–5).

13. a. Bassanio admits that he's "disabled his estate" and that an earlier loan from Antonio is now gone (I.i.130–31).

14. b. Don Pedro of Tuscany is the only gentleman not wooing Portia from afar.

15. c. A major reason that the Christians scorn Shylock is that he is a "usurer," that is, he breeds money, which the Christians consider sinful.

16. b. and c. The two suitors who appear to woo Portia are the Prince of Morocco and the Prince of Arragon.

17. a. Launcelot Gobbo does not appear in the Olivier film of the play.

18. d. All of the rhymes point to the correct casket.

19. a. Nerissa's engagement was a risk that Gratiano took: if Bassanio won Portia, he would win Nerissa. He says, "Your fortune stood upon the casket there . . . I got a promise of this fair one here/To have her love, provided that your fortune/Achiev'd her mistress"(III.ii.203–9).

20. b. Portia's travels to the court of Venice as Balthasar.

21. a. Olivier's howl as he exits the trial scene is truly remarkable. He says in his autobiography that to achieve this sound, he would throw himself on the floor backstage so violently that he would actually experience pain.

22. a. Portia requests Antonio's gloves, which are provided willingly, but she has to work a little harder to secure the ring from Bassanio.

Much Ado About Nothing

23. a. In Shakespeare's day, "nothing" was pronounced much like "noting." The pun is appropriate because the motif of noting is apparent: Benedick notes Beatrice, Claudio notes Hero, Balthasar and Don Pedro jest about notes: "Note, notes, forsooth, and nothing" (II.iii.59).

24. c. In Branagh's film, Emma Thompson is reading aloud the song from act 2, scene 3, which begins, "Sigh no more, ladies, sigh no more, / Men were deceivers ever . . ."

25. b. In the Branagh film Don Pedro's bastard brother Don John is played by Keanu Reeves.

26. c. Conrade and Borachio are Don John's accomplices who execute the plot slandering Hero.

27. b. Although the content of the conversation with the Prince and Claudio is misunderstood by Antonio's man (I.ii.9–12), the truth is that the Prince vows to woo Hero for Claudio (I.i.310–12).

28. a. From afar Claudio sees a scene that he believes to be Hero and an unknown lover, but this is a trick. He actually is watching Borachio and Margaret.

29. c. Beatrice is so angry Claudio has rejected her cousin that she insists that if Benedick really loves her, he will kill Claudio (IV.i.291).

30. b. When Hero's virtue is revealed and she has supposedly died, Claudio says, "Impose me to what penance your invention / Can lay upon my sin" (V.i.283–84). Leonato tells him,

"Possess the people in Messina here
How innocent she died; and if your love
Can harbour aught in sad invention,
Hang her an epitaph upon her tomb" (V.i.291–94).

31. a. True love develops through time, trial, and trust. The difference between the courtship of Benedick and Beatrice and that of Claudio and Hero is that the former takes place over time, the testing of loyalty, and the trusting of each other's word: on the other hand, Claudio and Hero's courtship is rapid and superficial and, consequently, almost unravels.

32. c. The Messenger portrays Claudio, who has behaved bravely in the war (I.i.13–15).

33. d Claudio rejects Hero at the altar with this cruel speech (IV.i.33–37).

34. e. The comic Dogberry describes the headborough Verges in this fashion (III.v.35–36).

35. a. Benedick depicts Beatrice in these terms (II.i.254–60).

36. b. Don Pedro's speech portrays Benedick comically (IV.ii.10–14).

Twelfth Night

37. c. The twelfth night of the title refers to the twelfth night after Christmas, the Feast of the Epiphany, when the three Magi arrived in Bethlehem with gifts for the newborn Christ child.

38. b. Olivia has vowed to keep her face veiled and to mourn her brother for seven years.

39. a. Cesario is the name that Viola chooses for her disguise.

40. c. Sir Toby Belch is Olivia's uncle.

41. e. The only one of the group who is not enamored of Olivia is Antonio. Orsino has attempted various strategies to win Olivia; Malvolio has yearned secretly for her; Sebastian falls in love with her at first sight; and Sir Andrew Aguecheek has been trying to buy her love.

42. b. One of the statements of the play is that young people should enjoy life while they are young. Another phrase to describe this attitude is *carpe diem,* which means "seize the day."

43.–46. At the end of the play the happy couples include (43) Olivia and Sebastian (e and g); (44) Orsino and Viola (f and h); and (45) Sir Toby Belch and Maria (b and d). The losers are (46) Sir Andrew Aguecheek and Malvolio (a and c).

47. a. This is a description of Sir Andrew Aguecheek by Sir Toby Belch (I.iii.25–27).

48. f. Malvolio describes the disguised Viola in this manner (I.v.164–67).

49. d. Malvolio is characterized by Maria (II.iii.159–63).

50. c. In this speech Feste, the clown, is viewed by Viola (III.i.67–72).

51. e. The mournful Olivia is pictured by Orsino's man, Valentine (I.i.26–30).

Dreams

52. l. King Richard III in *Richard III* awakes from a prophetic nightmare of the coming battle and recognizes the villainy of his life (V.iii.177–79).

53. h. Hermia in *A Midsummer Night's Dream* has an intu-

itive dream that her lover, Lysander, is cruel to her (II.ii.147–50).

54. k. In *Romeo and Juliet,* Mercutio describes the nature of dreams (I.iv.96–100).

55. e. Cleopatra in *Antony and Cleopatra* mourns the loss of her great love in terms of a dream (V.ii.76–78).

56. j. King Henry V, formerly Falstaff's friend and comrade in mischief, now rejects Falstaff in favor of his royal commitment (2 Henry IV.V.v.52–55).

57. d. In *Richard III,* George, Duke of Clarence, has a terrifying nightmare that presages his death (I.iv.2–6).

58. b. Bottom has been magically turned into an ass by Oberon, but the experience has been made into a pleasantly luxuriant dream for him by Titania and her fairies (IV.i.208–11).

59 i. In *Julius Caesar,* Caesar recounts Calpurnia's prophetic dream of his assassination and refuses, at first, to appear in the senate (II.ii.76–79).

60. c. In *The Tempest,* Caliban relates the wonderful dreams he had that promised riches beyond belief (III.ii.149–52).

61. g. Hamlet's torment comes through in his dreams (II.ii.260–61).

62. a. Antigonus in *The Winter's Tale,* ordered to abandon Hermione's baby in some desert place, dreams that the dead Hermione has appeared to him and means for him to leave the baby in Bohemia (III.iii.16–22).

63. f. The Doctor in *Macbeth* infers that Lady Macbeth's sleepwalking indicates a troubled mind and not an illness (V.i.79–82).

All's Well that Ends Well

64. a. They are mourning Bertram's father, the Countess's husband, who has recently passed away.

65. b. Bertram is an extremely self-centered young man; many wonder that Helena yearns so for him.

66. c. Parolles, a follower of Bertram, is a liar, fool, and coward, which he makes plain through the play, and he is described so by Helena (I.i.111–12).

67. b. Helena, using the skill taught her by her father, Gerard de Narbon, cures the King of his mysterious disease.

68. a. Helena states this theme best in her soliloquy, which begins, "Our remedies oft in ourselves do lie;/which we ascribe to heaven" (I.i.231–32).

69. c. The token that Bertram demands is his ring which he claims will never come off his finger (III.ii.59–60).

70. b. The action is to "show me a child begotten of thy body that I am father to" (III.ii.61–62). Only then will he accept her as his wife.

71. b. Helena is substituted for Diana in the assignation with Bertram.

72. c. Parolles is revealed as the coward he is by boasting that he will recover the company's drum.

73. a. True. Since Helena has managed to perform the two tasks Bertram set for her, Bertram promises to love her "ever, ever dearly" (V.iii.317).

b. True. The King promises Diana a dowry for any husband she chooses.

c. False. Parolles is disgraced and ostracized, but not officially banished.

Measure for Measure

74. a. The Duke is describing Angelo to the Friar as he explains the reasons he has left Angelo in power in Vienna (I.iii.51–53).

75. b. Claudio and Julietta, lacking a dowry, consummated their love. Now, he says, "Our most mutual entertainment/ With character too gross is writ on Juliet" (I.ii.157–58). In other words, she's pregnant.

76. c. The conflict is whether a strict interpretation of the law, representing justice, is preferable to one that considers all circumstances and perhaps might dispense mercy.

77. c. Lucio is speaking to Isabella, assuring her that he respects her state as a novice(I.iv.37–40).

78. a. In prison, Pompey makes a deal for his freedom by agreeing to help the executioner (IV.ii.16).

79. a. A "fantastic," according to Webster's, is one who has fanciful ideas or presents an "unrestrained extravagance of conception."

80. b. In the bed trick Mariana slips in by the garden gate and beds with Angelo, as a substitute for Isabella.

81. c. *Cucullus non facit monachum* translates as "a cowl [a hood] does not make a monk," which Lucio declares, with unconscious irony (V.i.263).

82. a. Isabel argues that although Claudio desired to sleep with her, and thought he had, in fact, he really hadn't, so thus should receive mercy. She says, "His act did not o'ertake his bad intent,/And must be buried but as an intent (V.i.456–57).

83.   a. False. Barnardine is forgiven and handed over to the Friar who will advise him (V. i.488–91).
       b. True. The Duke tells Claudio to "restore her" and

wishes her joy (V.1.531). We can assume that means Claudio will marry her.

c. False. Ragozine dies in prison of natural causes (IV.iii.71–74).

d. True. The Duke forgives Lucio's slandering him, but he does insist that "any woman wrong'd by this lewd fellow . . . he shall marry her" (V.i.514, 518). "Marrying a 'punk,'" says Lucio, is "pressing to death, whipping and hanging" (V.i.528–29).

Troilus and Cressida

84. a. In the first speech of the play, the Prologue announces, "Troyan and Greek / Sets all on hazard, and hither am I come, a Prologue arm'd" (Prol.21–23).

85. d. Diomedes is not one of Troilus's brothers. The others are all sons of Priam, and thus Troilus's siblings.

86. a. Pandarus says, "He that will have a cake out of the wheat must needs tarry the grinding . . . the bolting . . . the leavening . . . the kneading, the making of the cake, the heating of the oven and the baking; nay, you must stay the cooling too, or you may chance to burn your lips" (I.i.15–25). He is speaking of Troilus's pursuit of Cressida.

87. b. Ulysses, in the great debate among the Greeks, declares that when a leader does not display the authority that is his, others who may be beneath him seem equal to him (when they are not) (I.iii.83–84).

88. c. As Ulysses's speech continues, he seems to be saying that the person most responsible for the Greeks' failure is Agamemnon.

89. a. Taste and food images run throughout the play as metaphors for idealistic love followed by disillusion. According to Caroline Spurgeon (*Shakespeare's Imagery,* Cambridge Univer-

sity Press, 1971), fourteen of the characters make use of food imagery, and there are forty-four such images in the play, from Pandarus's advice about "the making of the cake" (I.i.23–24), to Troilus's depiction of Cressida as "food for fortune's tooth," (IV.v. 293) to his disillusion at her betrayal with Diomedes when he cries bitterly,

> "The fractions of her faith, orts of her love,
> The fragments, scraps, the bits and greasy relics
> Of her o'er-eaten faith, are bound to Diomed." (V.ii.158–160)

90. c. The death of Patroclus, together with the mangled Myrmidons, energizes Achilles; he arms and goes into battle, seeking Hector and vowing vengeance.

91. c. Cressida bemoans the fact that when men court a woman, she is very special, like an angel; but when they have won her, the wooing stops (I.ii.312–13).

92. h. Ulysses in this great speech declares that when order is not kept, and hierarchy not respected, the result will be failure (I.iii.101–3).

93. g. Troilus is speaking about the value of Helen (II.ii.81–82).

94. e. Pandarus (III.i.143–145).

95. f. Thersites enunciates the themes of the play (V.ii.195–196).

96. d. Nestor argues that men are proven to be men with their behavior in misfortune (I.iii.33–34).

97. g. Troilus argues that value resides in what is thought to be valuable (II.ii.52).

98. b. Cassandra prophesies the coming disaster (II.ii.101–2).

99. a. Agamemnon manipulates Ajax who doesn't realize he's being described (II.iii.165–68).

100. a. False. Cressida is with Diomedes.

101. b. True. Hector has been killed by Achilles, his body tied to the horse's tail and dragged around the field of battle.

102. c. False. Troilus is alive but grief-stricken at Cressida's betrayal.

Music

101. The passage comes from *The Two Gentlemen of Verona*, and the speaker is Proteus who is giving advice to the Duke how Thurio, the Duke's preferred lover, should behave to win the love of Sylvia (III.ii.78–81).

102. In prison, *Richard II* regrets the waste of his life and likens it to music being played without respect to time or proportion (V.v.41-44).

103. Peter banters with the musicians in *Romeo and Juliet*, who have been hired to play for Juliet's wedding, but now find that she is believed dead and they might as well go home. But Peter wants music; they refuse, and a quarrel results (IV.v.141–45).

104. This well-known passage is spoken by Lorenzo in *The Merchant of Venice* as he tells Jessica of the power of music to calm the nature both of beasts and men (V.i.83–88).

105. Duke Orsino in *Twelfth Night,* languishing in an excess of love, seeks music to feed upon and satisfy his craving (I.i.1–7).

106. The Duke, disguised as a priest in *Measure for Measure,* offers philosophy to Mariana, who has begged his forgiveness for appearing frivolous with her music (IV.i.14–15).

107. This is another passage that views music as a food for lovers. Here Cleopatra, in *Antony and Cleopatra,* yearns for the comfort of Antony's return from Rome (II.v. 1–2).

108. In *Cymbeline,* Cloten attempts to bring Imogen forth from her room with music (II.iii.31–34).

109. In *The Tempest,* as he laments his father's probable death, Ferdinand hears magical music, which calms the waters and his passion alike (I.ii.387–93).

110. And from the same play, Caliban describes to Stephano and Trinculo the "sounds and sweet airs" that he hears on the island (III.ii.144–52).

ACT IV

Major Players

So now you're a Major Player; like an actor, you've graduated from the amateur, apprentice and professional levels into the ranks of those who assume major roles because they have experience and knowledge and talent. Majors have paid their dues—they may be teachers of Shakespeare, either in secondary or collegiate institutions; they may be lead actors in an acting company; or they may not be actors or academics at all, but patrons of the theater and passionate about these particular plays. This was the goal, wasn't it, to be a Major Player, perhaps even an MVP?

Shakespeare became a Major Player about 1600. In an astonishing burst of creativity between 1601 and 1608, he produced, after *Hamlet,* four masterpieces, and two fine plays. He was at the peak of his powers and clearly a "major player" in the London theater scene.

Since you're a Major Player—you're obviously primed for the major plays. And now's the time to accompany Shakespeare through this period of his life and career, beginning with a broad quiz about scenes, settings, and speeches, continuing with questions about *Hamlet, Othello, King Lear, Macbeth, Antony and Cleopatra, Coriolanus,* and *Timon of Athens,* and ending with a quiz about heroines and Hamlets, a recognition of the women who have contributed memorable performances through the centuries.

There are 195 questions in the major players section and the answers begin on page 156. If you score 100 or more, you're certified a Major Player. The next question is "To Be or Not to Be" a Superstar.

Scenes, Settings, and Speeches

To begin as a Major Player, try these scenes, but don't get too sure of yourself. Most of the questions refer to plays already covered, though some do not.

1. "The Willow Scene" refers to

    a. Ophelia's drowning in the creek in *Hamlet*
    b. Rosalind's encounter with Orlando underneath a willow tree in the Forest of Arden in *As You Like It*
    c. Desdemona's preparation for bed in *Othello*

2. The "bed trick" is not used in

    a. *Measure for Measure*
    b. *Much Ado About Nothing*
    c. *All's Well That Ends Well*

3. "The Brothel Scene" refers to

    a. the scene in the tavern with Hal and Falstaff in *1 Henry IV*
    b. the scene in *Othello* in which Othello treats Desdemona like a whore
    c. the scene in *Pericles* in which Marina is brought to the bawd.

4. "The Mousetrap" refers to

   a. Oberon's method of tricking Titania in *Midsummer Night's Dream*
   b. the trick Isabella plays on Angelo in *Measure for Measure*
   c. the play that Hamlet arranges for Claudius in *Hamlet*

5. In what play does an incriminating scene viewed from afar *not* occur?

   a. *Othello*
   b. *All's Well That Ends Well*
   c. *Troilus and Cressida*
   d. *Much Ado About Nothing*

6. The "Temptation Scene" refers to

   a. Poins's tempting Hal to rob the pilgrims in *1 Henry IV*
   b. Iago's tempting Emilia to steal Desdemona's handkerchief in *Othello*
   c. Iago's tempting Othello into the belief that Desdemona is unfaithful

7. The "Closet Scene" refers to

   a. the scene between Hamlet and Gertrude in her bedroom
   b. the scene between Othello and Desdemona in her bedroom
   c. the scene between Macbeth and Lady Macbeth when they plan Duncan's murder

No evidence exists that Shakespeare ever traveled outside of England, and his choice of settings for the plays usually derives from his sources. Still, his active imagination accepted the settings in many places in Europe and in the Mediterranean countries and developed them for his own purposes.

As some plays have more than one setting, match the more significant location to the play.

Play

a. *Antony and Cleopatra* e. *Much Ado About Nothing*
b. *Hamlet*   f. *Othello*
c. *Julius Caesar*   g. *Timon of Athens*
d. *Macbeth*   h. *Troilus and Cressida*

Location

  8. Athens   _____
  9. Alexandria _____
10. Cyprus   _____
11. Denmark   _____
12. Messina   _____
13. Rome   _____
14. Scotland   _____
15. Troy   _____

The following speeches describe one of these characters:

a. Antony   f. Desdemona
b. Brutus   g. Hamlet
c. Cassio   h. Lear
d. Cleopatra   i. Macbeth
e. Cordelia   j. Othello

16. "A maiden never bold:
    Of spirit so still and quiet, that her motion
    Blush'd at herself."

                          _____

17. "O, what a noble mind is here o'erthrown!
    The courtier, soldier's, scholar's, eye, tongue, sword:
    Th'expectancy and rose of the fair state,
    The glass of fashion and the mould of form."

    _____

18.   "Her voice was ever soft,
    Gentle, and low, an excellent thing in woman."

    _____

19.   "Is this the nature
    Whom passion could not shake? whose solid virtue
    The shot of accident, nor dart of chance,
    Could neither graze nor pierce?"

    _____

20.   "For her own person,
    It beggar'd all description; she did lie
    In her pavilion—cloth-of-gold of tissue—
    O'er-picturing that Venus where we see
    The fancy outwork nature."

    _____

21. "This was the noblest Roman of them all.
    . . . His life was gentle, and the elements
    So mix'd in him that Nature might stand up
    And say to all the world: 'This was a man.' "

    _____

22.   "A Florentine,
    A man almost damn'd in a fair wife;
    That never set a squadron in the field,
    Nor the division of a battle knows
    More than a spinster."

    _____

23. "'Tis the infirmity of his age; yet he hath ever but
slenderly known himself."

_____

24. "His legs bestrid the ocean; his rear'd arm
Crested the world; his voice was propertied
As all the tuned spheres, and that to friends;
But when he meant to quail and shake the orb,
He was as rattling thunder."

_____

25. "Some say he's mad; others that lesser hate him
Do call it valiant fury: but, for certain,
He cannot buckle his distemper'd cause
Within the belt of rule."

_____

Hamlet

Both the play *Hamlet* and the role of Hamlet are considered by many the greatest in Western literature. Young actors dream about playing Hamlet and it's a must for an actor of stature.

Try these questions about the play, actors of the role, and films produced.

26. Before the play begins, the Ghost of Hamlet's father has
been seen by Bernardo and Marcellus, the sentinels of the
castle,

   a. once
   b. twice
   c. three times

27. The university that Hamlet attended was

    a. the University of Heidelberg
    b. Oxford University
    c. the University of Wittenberg

28. The name of the castle in *Hamlet* is

    a. Inverness
    b. Elsinore
    c. Blenheim

29. The Ghost of Hamlet's father commands him to

    a. avenge his foul and most unnatural murder
    b. avenge his defeat on the plains of Norway
    c. leave Ophelia to the powers above

30. Ophelia returns Hamlet's gifts because

    a. Polonius tells her to
    b. Gertrude is jealous of their relationship
    c. she wants their relationship to move more slowly

31. The reason the players have arrived at the castle is

    a. Hamlet promised them a large sum of money for putting on a special play that would prove Claudius's guilt
    b. the plague is rampant in the city and they had to get out
    c. the boys' company is so fashionable the adult actors had to go on tour

32. Hamlet stabs Polonius

    a. in his mother's bedroom
    b. in the orchard where his father was poisoned
    c. in the hall behind the throne room

33. The "occasion" prompting Hamlet's soliloquy that begins

"How all occasions do inform against me
And spur my dull revenge!" (IV.iv 32–33)

    a. is the sight of Ophelia in her casket
    b. is the sight of Fortinbras's army marching to Poland
    c. is the sight of Gertrude and Claudius making love
       behind the arras

34. In the Closet Scene (III.iv), Hamlet shows Gertrude

    a. his father's sword
    b. his father's last will and testament
    c. pictures of his father and Claudius

35. One of the flowers that the mad Ophelia does *not* mention is

    a. pansies
    b. fennel
    c. forget-me-nots
    d. daisies

36. The age of Hamlet when he returns from England is

    a. twenty-one
    b. twenty-seven
    c. thirty

37. Poisons are used or referred to in many instances of the play and may signify the corruption of the state. Identify the one poison that is *not* used:

   a. the poison used to kill old Hamlet
   b. the poison that Ophelia drinks before drowning in the creek
   c. the poison used on the sword to kill Hamlet
   d. the poison in the drink that Gertrude mistakenly drinks

38. The character left to tell Hamlet's story is

   a. Osric
   b. Horatio
   c. Marcellus

39. The number of people who die during or by the end of the play (not including the Ghost of Hamlet's father) is

   a. five
   b. eight
   c. ten

40.–45. The passage below is the most familiar in all English literature. It also is a remarkable example of Shakespeare's skill with language. Fill in the blanks with Shakespeare's choices, if you can; but, failing that, select your own and compare your choices with his. Score yourself half a point for each of Shakespeare's choices.

"To be or not to be, that is the (40) _____ :
Whether 'tis nobler in the mind to _____
The (41) _____ and arrows of outrageous fortune,
Or to take _____ against a sea of (42) _____ ,
And by _____ , end them? To (43) _____ ; to sleep;
No more; and by a sleep to say we_____
The (44) _____ and the thousand _____ shocks
That (45) _____ is heir to; 'tis a consummation
_____ to be wish'd."

Actors of *Hamlet*

All of the actors below have been considered outstanding
by their contemporaries in the role of Hamlet. Match the speaker
to the speech.

a. John Barrymore   f. Richard Burbage
b. Thomas Betterton   g. Richard Burton
c. William Henry West Betty   h. Edwin Forrest
d. Edwin Booth   i. David Garrick
e. Kenneth Branagh   j. Laurence Olivier

46. My five foot four height always bothered me, so when I
    played Hamlet I wore shoes with platform heels to add to
    it. I also wired my hat (they say) so that when I saw the
    Ghost it would fall off and my hair stand on end. I made
    some judicious cuts in the play and provided a more
    positive ending to the play. Although some deplored my
    alterations, I was considered the greatest Hamlet of the
    eighteenth century.

    _____

47. In my film I set the "To be or not to be" speech in a great
    mirrored hall. I wanted to convey the Wittenberg frame
    of mind, which would be intellectual and reflective. So

I don't move, although there is a fast cut to Claudius and Polonius who seem to be eavesdropping.

---

48. I was thirteen when I played Hamlet in London in 1804–05. I was a very remarkable young man and very popular for two seasons, but the public turned against me and hissed me off the stage in 1807.

---

49. I played the first Hamlet. I was the leading actor of the Globe company and played most of the leading tragic roles. I was so good as Richard III that backstage actors called me "King Dick." Still, Hamlet was my principal role, and one of my contemporaries wrote that when I seemed to bleed at the end of the play, not only the spectators but also my fellow actors thought perhaps I had in fact died. My tombstone identifies me as Hamlet.

---

50. I was the first great American Hamlet. However, I am more often remembered for the rivalry with William Macready over performances of Macbeth that precipitated the Astor Place Riot of 1848 in which twenty-two people were killed.

---

51. I was the great Hamlet of the Restoration and was skillful enough as an actor to turn pale at the appearance of the Ghost in the closet scene. I was the first actor to be interred in Westminster Abbey.

---

52. As Hamlet, I was described as "every inch the noble prince and true born gentleman." Interested in spirituality, I emphasized Hamlet's devotion to his father, and sometimes on stage imagined I heard my own father's voice in that of the Ghost.

_____

53. In my film I played the "To be or not to be" speech from a rock overlooking the sea. It seemed to me the most natural thing in the world to have Hamlet's soliloquy as words in his head.

_____

54. I was at Oxford when I saw Gielgud's Hamlet. He made such a magnificent gesture on the line "When we have shuffled off this mortal coil" that the friend I was with completely gave up drinking. Years later I played Hamlet successfully on Broadway while I was married to Elizabeth Taylor.

_____

55. Called by some the greatest Hamlet of my era, I emphasized Hamlet's masculinity. I said, "I want him to be so male that when I come out on stage they can hear my balls clank."

_____

Hamlet on **Film**

Many directors and actors of the twentieth century have dedicated themselves to producing films of *Hamlet*.

56. An actor who has *not* played *Hamlet* on film is

    a. Kevin Kline
    b. Nicol Williamson
    c. Al Pacino
    d. Mel Gibson
    e. Ethan Hawke

57. In Franco Zeffirelli's film, the first scene shows

    a. Bernardo and Marcellus shivering around a fire
    b. Gertrude weeping over her first husband's tomb
    c. a huge metal statue coming to life

58. The "To be or not to be" speech is played by this Hamlet in the Action aisle of a Blockbuster video store by

    a. Kenneth Branagh
    b. Laurence Olivier
    c. Ethan Hawke

59. The famous Hollywood actor who plays the Player King in Branagh's film is

    a. Clint Eastwood
    b. Gregory Peck
    c. Charlton Heston

60. Olivier chose to use black and white photography in his film because

   a. Technicolor film was not available at the time
   b. he wanted to use deep focus
   c. he thought that his skin tones didn't work well in the color available at the time

61. The *Hamlet* filmed in nineteenth-century dress is

   a. Franco Zeffirelli's
   b. Kenneth Branagh's
   c. Laurence Olivier's
   d. Michael Almereyda's
   e. Tony Richardson's

62. The film version in which Rosencrantz, Guildenstern, and Fortinbras are cut is

   a. Tony Richardson's
   b. Kenneth Branagh's
   c. Laurence Olivier's
   d. Franco Zeffirelli's

63. Arrange their *Hamlet* films in chronological order:

   a. Franco Zeffirelli–Mel Gibson
   b. Kenneth Branagh
   c. Michael Almereyda–Ethan Hawke
   d. Laurence Olivier
   e. Tony Richardson–Nicol Williamson

64. Match the film Ophelias with their respective Hamlets:

   a. Kenneth Branagh   c. Ethan Hawke
   b. Mel Gibson   d. Laurence Olivier

1. Helena Bonham Carter _____
2. Jean Simmons _____
3. Julia Stiles _____
4. Kate Winslet _____

65. This one is tougher. Match the actors who played Claudius with their Gertrudes:

    a. Julie Christie   d. Judy Parfitt
    b. Glenn Close   e. Diane Venora
    c. Eileen Herlie

1. Alan Bates _____
2. Anthony Hopkins _____
3. Derek Jacobi _____
4. Kyle Maclachlin _____
5. Basil Sydney _____

Othello

66. In act 1, scene 1, Iago is disgruntled because

    a. Othello didn't name him lieutenant
    b. Cassio has been after his wife, Emilia
    c. Othello accused him of misusing company funds

67. "Making the beast with two backs" refers to

    a. Iago's clay model of two horses
    b. Emilia's deformed child
    c. Othello and Desdemona making love

68. When Iago speaks of "the immediate jewel of their souls,"
he is referring to a man and woman's

   a. chastity
   b. good name
   c. religious faith

69. The one fact that Iago has to support his web of lies about
Desdemona is

   a. she lied to her father
   b. he saw Cassio wipe his beard with Desdemona's
      handkerchief
   c. Cassio dreamed of Desdemona and spoke her name

70. When Othello says, "This argues fruitfulness and liberal
heart," he is referring to

   a. Desdemona's low-cut dress
   b. Desdemona's moist palm
   c. Desdemona's pleading for Cassio

71. Desdemona learned the Willow Song from

   a. her mother, who used to sing her to sleep with it
   b. her no-good brother
   c. her mother's maid, Barbary

72. The adjective used to describe Iago many times is

   a. brave
   b. honest
   c. loyal

73. According to Othello, the sibyl who sewed the handkerchief with the strawberries was

    a. two hundred years old
    b. a thousand years old
    c. fifty years old

74. At the end of the play, the person left in charge of Cyprus is

    a. Lodovico
    b. Cassio
    c. Montano

Identify the character described in these speeches:

75. "The knave is handsome, young, and hath all those requisites in him that folly and green minds look after."

    _____

76. "This fellow's of exceeding honesty,
And knows all qualities, with a learned spirit,
Of human dealings."

    _____

77. "A housewife that by selling her desires
Buys herself bread and clothes."

    _____

78. "The gravity and stillness of your youth
The world hath noted, and your name is great
In mouths of gravest censure."

    _____

79.–82. True or False. (Score yourself half a point for each correct answer.)

    a. Othello's family has all been lowly born. _____

    b. Brabantio claims that Desdemona has always been a rather bold, venturous girl. _____

    c. Cassio tells Iago that he is a rather poor drinker. _____

    d. Iago urges Cassio to seek Desdemona's help in getting forgiveness from Othello. _____

    e. Desdemona tells Cassio she would rather die than give up his cause. _____

    f. Othello's first plan to kill Desdemona is to stab her with a dagger. _____

    g. Iago tells Roderigo that under the orders brought from Venice Othello is to go to Mauritania. _____

    h. Emilia is slain by Othello. _____

Othello on Film

Although perhaps not as well known as the *Hamlet* films, *Othello* has been produced a number of times on film, with actors such as Laurence Fishburne, John Kani, Orson Welles, and Willard White in the title role. Don't be surprised if your IQ fails you here.

83. Name the title of the film adaptation of *Othello* that is set in an American high school in the South.

    _____

84. Here is a real test of your skill as a Major Player. Name the actor who plays Othello in an independent film of *Othello* who achieved later fame as Inspector Giardello in the TV series *Homicide*. (His name is not mentioned above.)

    _____

85. Here you have a choice. Name the actor who commented about his film performance that "films based on obvious stage origins sometimes misfire . . . my performance was tired. I mistimed effects."

    a. Ian McKellen
    b. Laurence Olivier
    c. Orson Welles
    d. Laurence Fishburne

86. Name the director whose *Othello*, originally produced in 1952–53, was thought to be lost until a print was found in New Jersey in 1991, and the film rereleased.

    _____

87. Which director of *Othello* costumed the film in mid-nineteenth-century dress, with Roderigo in the opening scene in a three-piece suit and hat?

    a. Janet Suzman
    b. Oliver Parker
    c. Trevor Nunn
    d. Orson Welles

88. Which director opened with a shot of a gondola on a Venetian canal, and a character holding the mask of tragedy over his face?

    a. Stewart Burge
    b. Oliver Parker
    c. Janet Suzman
    d. Orson Welles

89. Whose opening for the film is a shot of the mourning procession for Othello and Desdemona as Iago is hoisted in a metal cage on the castle walls?

    a. Suzman-Kani's
    b. Parker-Fishburne's
    c. Welles's
    d. Burge-Olivier's

90. Whose Othello commits suicide with an African fetish?

    a. Orson Welles's
    b. John Kani's
    c. Willard White's
    d. Laurence Fishburne's

91. Whose Iago has a small dog?

    a. Kenneth Branagh's
    b. Michael MacLiammoir's
    c. Richard Hadden Haines's
    d. Ian McKellen's

92.–96. Match the Othellos with their Iagos.

    a. Kenneth Branagh   d. Michael MacLiammoir
    b. Frank Finlay   e. Ian McKellen
    c. Richard Hadden Haines

92. Laurence Fishburne _____

93. John Kani _____

94. Laurence Olivier _____

95. Orson Welles _____

96. Willard White _____

King Lear

97. The first lines of the play, "I thought the King had more affected the Duke of Cornwall than Albany," set up the theme of

   a. excess vs. moderation
   b. individual value and worth
   c. justice and mercy

98. What is the question that Lear asks his daughters?

   _____

99. Of Lear's three daughters, the one who answers, "Nothing," is

   a. Goneril
   b. Regan
   c. Cordelia

100. In his soliloquy, Edmund expresses anger at

   a. a society that deprives him of status because of his illegitimacy
   b. his father who wouldn't send him to a good school
   c. his brother, who is handsomer and brighter

101. The Fool's function in the play is to

   a. provide entertainment for Lear
   b. tell him the truth no matter how angry Lear gets
   c. protect him from his daughters

102. When Kent is banished, he disguises himself by

    a. dressing like a peasant and carrying a scythe
    b. shaving off his beard
    c. wearing a false nose and painting a scar on his cheek

103. When Edgar flees, he disguises himself as

    a. an itinerant priest, selling relics of the True Cross
    b. slick Sly, the merchant, selling cures for syphilis
    c. Poor Tom Turlygod, a Bedlam beggar

104. In the quarrel over the number of Lear's servants, Regan at first offers to take

    a. five and twenty
    b. fifty
    c. seventy and five

105. Gloucester is blinded by

    a. a hot poker
    b. Cornwall's foot
    c. Regan's nails

One of the motifs of the play develops around the uses of nature. Lear, Edmund, Gloucester, the Doctor, Kent, Regan, all speak of nature in some fashion. Identify the speakers of these quotations.

106. "Hear Nature, hear; dear goddess, hear!
    Suspend thy purpose, if thou didst intend
    To make this creature fruitful!"

107. "Thou, Nature, art my goddess, to thy law
My services are bound."

_____

108. "Nature in you stands on the very verge
Of her confine."

_____

109. "Is there any cause in nature that makes
these hard hearts?"

_____

110. "How, my lord, I may be censured, that
nature thus gives way to loyalty, something
fears me to think of."

_____

111. "Oppressed nature sleeps."

_____

112.   "Our foster-nurse of nature is repose,
The which he lacks."

_____

113. "O ruin'd piece of nature! This great world
Shall so wear out to nought."

_____

114.   "Thou hast one daughter,
Who redeems nature from the general curse
Which twain have brought her to."

_____

115. "I pant for life! some good I mean to do,
Despite of mine own nature."

_____

King Lear on Film

The films of *King Lear* are not as well known as those of *Hamlet* or *Macbeth*. Still, there are four outstanding film versions: two English, one Russian, and one Japanese. Match the filmmaker and actor with the description of the film. (Some films are used twice.)

    a. Michael Elliott and Laurence Olivier
    b. Peter Brook and Paul Scofield
    c. Grigori Kosintsev and Oleg Dal
    d. Akira Kurosawa and Tatsuya Nakadai

116. The opening shots are in a location that looks like Stonehenge. _____

117. In the long opening, peasants are converging on the castle to hear of the division of the kingdom. _____

118. The opening shots of this film picture Lear out hunting, preparing to shoot. _____

119. This film was influenced by Jan Kott's essay "King Lear or Endgame" (*Shakespeare Our Contemporary*, Doubleday, 1964). _____

120. Lear's kingdom is signified by a bundle of arrows, which is broken by the rebellious child. _____

121. In one of the mad scenes, Lear eviscerates and eats a rabbit. _____

122. With dramatic sound, Lear's cry of "Howl, howl, howl" sets up an echo against the castle walls and the hills beyond. _____

123. In this adaptation, a character leaves her brother to retrieve his beloved flute. We see her dead, the flute still in her hand. _____

124. At the end of this film, Lear looks up and falls slowly out of the frame. The screen goes to white. _____

125. The film ends with the weeping Fool, playing on his pipe. _____

Macbeth on Film

Macbeth has provided the material for several memorable films of the twentieth century, including those made by

    a. Orson Welles
    b. Trevor Nunn
    c. Roman Polanski
    d. Akira Kurasawa

Try to "beat the Bard" with these identifications.

126. This film was influenced by a previous stage production that was set in Haiti and used "voodoo" drums as background. _____

127. While three of the films are entitled *Macbeth,* the title of Kurasawa's film is

    a. *Blood on the Crown*
    b. *Throne of Blood*
    c. *Blood Royal*

128. In the opening of this film, the camera is high above a large circle with characters who move in unison to sit on stools. _____

129. In this film, there is only one witch. _____

130. In the opening of this film, the three witches make a clay effigy of Macbeth. _____

131. In this opening, the witches dig a circle in the sand into which they put in a hand, a noose, and a dagger, and then sprinkle blood over it. _____

132. This is the only film in which we actually see Macbeth murder Duncan. _____

133. This film uses a bare stage and contemporary costumes. _____

134. In Kurasawa's adaptation, Macbeth is killed by

    a. an ax
    b. a wild boar
    c. a plethora of arrows

135.–138. Match the Macbeths with their Lady Macbeths.

    a. Francesca Annis   c. Jeanette Nolan
    b. Judi Dench   d. Izuzu Yamada

135. Jon Finch   _____

136. Ian McKellen   _____

137. Toshiro Mifume   _____

138. Orson Welles   _____

139. Finally, a question from theatrical lore. Why is this play frequently referred to as "The Scottish play" rather than by its title?

Antony and Cleopatra

A vast and intense play, *Antony and Cleopatra* combines love and political struggle in its tragedy.

140. The time period of this play is

    a. about 40 B.C.
    b. about A.D. 600
    c. about A.D. 900

141. The Caesar in the play is

    a. Julius Caesar
    b. Julius Caesar's son
    c. Julius Caesar's grand-nephew

142. In act 1, scene 1, Philo describes Antony as a "triple pillar of the world transform'd/ Into a stumpet's fool." If Antony is one pillar, who are the other two?

    a. _____   b. _____

143. When Fulvia, his wife, dies, Antony

    a. marries Cleopatra in a magnificent ceremony
    b. buries her body at sea in a lead casket
    c. marries Caesar's sister, Octavia

144. One of Cleopatra's women is Charmian. The other is

    a. Octavia
    b. Iras
    c. Calpurnia

145. In the party scene on Pompey's galley in act 2, Menas suggests to Pompey that

    a. with a special potion he has they can drug the "three world-sharers" and cut their throats
    b. if Pompey will create a distraction, he will lead Antony to the bow of the ship and push him overboard
    c. he will cut the cables and then they can cut the throats of the "three world-sharers"

146. The decisive naval battle fought between Caesar and Antony takes place at

    a. Phillippi
    b. Actium
    c. Alexandria

147. In act 4, the stage direction reads *"Music of hautboys is heard under the stage."* It signifies

    a. the parting of Antony from Cleopatra
    b. the orchestra tuning up its instruments for the finale
    c. the god Hercules leaving Antony

148. After Antony does not accomplish his suicide efficiently, he

    a. boards a ship that will take him up the Nile
    b. has himself hoisted up the pyramid to Cleopatra
    c. has Eros staunch his wounds with mud so that he can survive

149.–156. Teachers of writing always urge their students to use strong verbs. Fill in Shakespeare's verb choices from the passage below and marvel at his skill.

a. become   e. hungry
b. bless   f. satisfies
c. cloy   g. stale
d. feed   h. wither

"Age cannot (149) _____ her, nor custom (150) _____ ,

Her infinite variety; other women (151) _____

The appetites they (152) _____ ; but she makes (153) ____

Where most she (154) _____ ; for vilest things

(155) _____ themselves in her; that the holy priests

(156) _____ her when she is riggish."

157. Name the famous stage and film couple, each a star, who played the title roles in *Antony and Cleopatra* and Shaw's *Caesar and Cleopatra* in repertory in London and New York in 1951.

Coriolanus

Coriolanus is one of the few plays (always excepting *Hamlet)* in which a mother's voice is heard.

158. The two groups in conflict in the play are

a. the Protestants and the Catholics
b. the Romans and the Etruscans
c. the patricians and the common people

159. Shakespeare turned to the ancient Roman republic for his tragic hero because

   a. he wanted a hero who, like Oedipus, was flawed by his desire to mate with his mother and kill his father
   b. he wanted a hero in high place who, through his pride and arrogance would fall from that high place
   c. he wanted a man strong enough to reject his wife and son in order to please his opponent, Aufidius, who offers him a more suitable world in which to demonstrate his remarkable skills in weaponry.

160. Menenius Agrippa explains the proper functioning of government for the general good by telling a "pretty tale," a fable, about the rebellion of the mutinous members of the body against

   a. the "kingly-crowned head"
   b. the "vigilant eye"
   c. the arm
   d. the "cormorant belly"
   e. the "trumpeter" tongue

161. Menenius Agrippa insults the First Citizen after telling his story by calling him

   a. "the basest bottom"
   b. "the Great Intestine"
   c. "Old Cock"
   d. "the littlest fingernail"
   e. "the great toe"
   f. "the heel"

162. Part of Caius Marcius's difficulty in attaining the rank of consul is

    a. his contempt for the commoners
    b. the rejection of Menenius's advice
    c. his continued admiration of the enemy of Rome, Aufidius
    d. his infidelity to his wife, Virgilia
    e. *a* and *c* but not *b* and *d*

163. Volumnia, Caius Marcius's mother, loves her son because he is

    a a peace-loving young man who honors his mother
    b. willing to live up to the manly picture of him in her mind
    c. reluctant to put on the gown of humility

164. Marcius earns the name of "Coriolanus" by

    a. taking the city of Corioli single-handedly when he is shut in alone
    b. threatening to kill any of his men who turn away from battle
    c. refusing to have his wounds bound up so Aufidius can see his bloody body and be afraid
    d. all of the above

165. Sicinius, the tribune, turns the citizens of Rome against Coriolanus by

    a. emphasizing Coriolanus's contempt for the common folk
    b. exposing Coriolanus as a coward
    c. locating the center of power in the senate instead of the marketplace

d. urging the people to seize the power that is
rightfully theirs ("What is the city but the people?")
e. *b* and *c* but not *a* and *d*
f. *a* and *d* but not *b* and *c*

166. At Volumnia's urging, Coriolanus returns to the
marketplace to apply for the position of consul, but
Sicinius and Brutus, the tribunes,

a. urge the people to banish Coriolanus as a traitor to
the people
b. demand that Coriolanus forfeit his crown received at
Corioli
c. demand that Coriolanus's name be struck from
every monument in Rome

167. As a result of the success of the tribunes, Coriolanus

a. promises to reform to the extent that he will show
his wounds in public
b. is tied to a great rock and rolled down the hill to the
Tiber river
c. banishes the city in a highly contemptuous speech

168. In his banishment, Coriolanus

a. turns himself over to Aufidius to be used as a
weapon against all enemies except Rome, because
Coriolanus could never raise a sword against his
home country
b. offers his throat to Aufidius to be cut or his sword in
vengeance
c. ends up on the Italian coastal island of Elbe like a
later exiled emperor
d. offers to fight for the Volscian state for forty pieces
of silver

169. In the Volscian camp before Rome, Coriolanus

 a. yields to Aufidius's demands that he sack Rome without pity
 b. turns his back on his new colleague and listens to his mother's pleas to spare Rome, thereby signing his death warrant at the hands (feet) of the angry Volscian troops
 c. hikes to the Tarpeian rock and throws himself from it

Timon of Athens

Although it stages well, *Timon of Athens* may not even have been finished and is considered Shakespeare's most misanthropic work.

170. A major theme of the play is

 a. the universality of human greed
 b. the tragic result of ambition
 c. the fickleness of fortune

171. Timon's great flaw is that

 a. he betrays the trust of his business associates
 b. he is extravagantly generous
 c. he is suspicious of mankind

172. Timon pays for the gifts he gives to his friends

 a. through loans
 b. with gold that he inherited from his father
 c. with land that he sells periodically

173. Apemantus, a churlish philosopher, claims that he does not want gifts from Timon because

    a. he himself is wealthy
    b. he thinks others are more worthy
    c. he refuses to be bribed into softening his railing

174. All but one are the excuses given by Timon's friends for not heeding his request for money.

    a. "This is no time to lend money"
    b. "I have no money right now"
    c. "The stars bode ill for me this month"
    d. "Must I be his last refuge?"

175. Alcibiades, an Athenian captain, appeals to the senate to

    a. forgive Timon's debts
    b. spare a friend's life
    c. provide funding to raise up an army

176. Timon's last feast in Athens consists of

    a. beef from his last cow and wine from the last of his reserves
    b. animal feed and milk
    c. boiling water and crockery

177. When Timon leaves Athens, he goes to

    a. a fishing village
    b. the Oracle at Delphi
    c. a cave near the seashore

178. Timon leaves Athens because

    a. his creditors have driven him from the city
    b. he wants to have nothing more to do with humanity
    c. he is planning a revolt against the senate

179. Timon digs because

    a. he wants to hide the gold his creditors have come
       after
    b. he's looking for a root to eat
    c. he wants to work the land so he does not have to
       depend on material goods

180. Timon's true friend is

    a. Apemantus
    b. Ventidius
    c. Flavius

181. The senators want Timon to return to Athens because

    a. they want to collect his gold
    b. the public has cried out for Timon to lead the country
    c. they want to halt Alcibiades' invasion

Heroines and Hamlets

Although male actors are generally the ones remembered for performances in Shakespeare, since the Restoration many women have also been major players, several even as Hamlet. There follow fourteen such stars. Match the speaker to the speech.

a. Dame Judith Anderson   h. Eleanora Duse
b. Dame Peggy Ashcroft   i. Uta Hagen
c. Charlotte Barnes   j. Fanny Kemble
d. Sarah Bernhardt   k. Hannah Pritchard
e. Charlotte Cushman   l. Sarah Siddons
f. Dame Judi Dench   m. Ellen Terry
g. Colleen Dewhurst   n. Dame Sybil Thorndike

182. In my sixties I toured America in the title role of *Hamlet.* Born in Australia, I played Gertrude on Broadway to John Gielgud's *Hamlet* in 1936, and a year later played Lady Macbeth to Olivier's Macbeth. I am probably the only actress to receive two Emmys for the same role: Lady Macbeth, which I played to Maurice Evans's Macbeth on television both in 1954 and 1960. I was knighted by Queen Elizabeth in 1960. _____

183. I have played at least eleven Shakespearean roles, the first as Desdemona to Paul Robeson's Othello, in 1930, when I was twenty-three. Two years later at the Old Vic, I played Rosalind in *As You Like It,* Perdita in *The Winter's Tale,* and Imogen in *Cymbeline.* I played many roles with John Gielgud for the next thirty years, including Beatrice, Ophelia, Titania, and Cordelia. In 1956 I was awarded a DBE, and by 1961 I was a member of the Royal Shakespeare Company (and later became a director), and also appeared with the company in *The War of The Roses* as Margaret of Anjou. _____

184. I astonished the world by playing the role of Hamlet at the age of fifty-five. I debuted at the age of eighteen at the Comédie Française in 1862 but did not achieve a notable success until I played Cordelia in *King Lear* ten years later. I am frequently identified with Rostand's *L'Aiglon*, which I played on many occasions. _____

185. Now a Dame of the British Empire, I debuted as Ophelia with John Neville at the Old Vic in 1957. I have played many of Shakespeare's characters, among them Beatrice, Viola, Lady Macbeth, and Cleopatra, and appeared as Mistress Quickly in Kenneth Branagh's *Henry V.* But it was as Elizabeth the Queen in the film *Shakespeare in Love* that I was awarded an Oscar. _____

186. I am known as England's greatest tragic actress and was immortalized by Joshua Reynolds in his painting *The Tragic Muse.* In my career I played fourteen of Shakespeare's females, but my interpretation of Lady Macbeth was my most triumphant. I rarely attempted comedy, and being a little prudish, I refused to wear man's attire in *As You Like It.* _____

187. Both my parents were actors and I first appeared on the stage when I was four. In my thirties I was well received in London when I performed the title role in *Hamlet*, but in general I was not accounted as good in male parts as my mother, who played Romeo to my Juliet. I am also the author of a number of plays, including *The Forest Princess,* based on the life of Pocahontas, and *Octavia Bragaldi,* based on a contemporary murder. _____

188. Sometimes considered the first great American actress, I began my career at nineteen singing the role of the Countess Almaviva in *The Marriage of Figaro.* But I lost my voice and was forced to turn to drama. I debuted in

1836 as Lady Macbeth. Because I possessed somewhat masculine features, I was successful in male roles, such as Hamlet, Oberon, and Cardinal Wolsey. I also played Romeo to my sister Susan's Juliet. In 1907 a club was established in my name in Philadelphia. _____

189. A niece of Sarah Siddons, I made my successful debut as Juliet at Covent Garden in 1829 at the age of nineteen, which helped to stave off bankruptcy for the theater. After an equally successful American tour, I married a Philadelphia slave owner, a marriage which ended in divorce in 1848. I am known as the author of *Journal of a Residence on a Georgia Plantation 1838–1839*, but I also pioneered the one-woman show, touring the northeast of America with readings of Shakespeare plays for twenty years. _____

190. An actress of the eighteenth century, I was much admired for my interpretations of Rosalind and Beatrice and other light roles, and played Nerissa to Kitty Clive's Portia in Charles Macklin's innovative production of *The Merchant of Venice.* In 1748 David Garrick invited me to join his company at Drury Lane where I remained as leading lady for twenty-one years. Although I played Gertrude and Queen Katherine in *Henry VIII,* I was truly outstanding as Lady Macbeth, and after I retired, Garrick never played Macbeth again. _____

191. My career began in 1904 with a wide variety of Shakespearean roles. During World War I, with the shortage of men, I played Prince Hal in *Henry IV,* Puck in *Midsummer Night's Dream,* the Fool in *King Lear,* Ferdinand in *The Tempest,* and Launcelot Gobbo in *The Merchant of Venice.* During World War II, I toured with the Old Vic, playing Lady Macbeth. _____

192. I first appeared on the English stage at the age of nine, in the role of Mamillius, in *The Winter's Tale,* with Charles Kean's company. In 1878 I was engaged as a leading lady at the Lyceum by Henry Irving, where I remained for twenty-five years, playing Ophelia, Beatrice, Desdemona, Juliet, and Imogen. After my third marriage failed, I toured America and Australia, giving readings and lectures of Shakespeare. My correspondence with George Bernard Shaw has been published and enjoyed. _____

193. My handbook, *Respect for Acting,* has been read by several generations of acting students. I played Ophelia to Eva Le Gallienne's Hamlet in 1937, and in 1943 was Desdemona to Paul Robeson's Othello. _____

194. Although I may be better known as an interpreter of the roles of Eugene O'Neill, at the New York Shakespeare Festival I played Tamora in *Titus Andronicus,* Katherine in *The Taming of the Shrew,* Lady Macbeth, Cleopatra, and Gertrude. The awards I received during my career were two Obies, two Tonys, four Emmys (one for playing Candice Bergen's mom), and two Geminis. _____

195. I was introduced to the Italian public at the age of four, and played Juliet at fourteen. In 1891, as an adult, I toured Russia, where Chekhov was so enchanted by my Cleopatra he may have been thinking of me when he wrote the role of Madame Arkadina in *The Seagull.* My style of acting was often contrasted with Sarah Bernhardt's; mine was more subtle and natural. I did not like to wear makeup onstage because I had the ability to blush or turn pale at will. _____

Answers

Scenes, Settings, and Speeches

1. c. The "Willow Scene" refers to the scene in which Desdemona, preparing for bed with Emilia's help, sings the "Willow Song," which she remembers sung by a maid of her mother's who died singing it (IV.iii.).

2. b. The "bed trick," in which one woman is substituted for another, unbeknownst to the man, is used both in *Measure for Measure* and *All's Well that Ends Well*. It does not occur in *Much Ado About Nothing*.

3. b. Act 4, scene 2 of *Othello* begins with Othello's treating Emilia like the madam of a brothel. He dismisses her with an abrupt "Some of your function, mistress; / Leave procreants alone and shut the door" (27–29). Thereafter he berates Desdemona in the foulest terms possible, accusing her of being a whore.

4. c. "The Mousetrap" is the play that Hamlet arranges for the court to evoke a guilty reaction from Claudius (III.ii).

5. b. *All's Well That Ends Well* is the only play in which an eavesdropping scene does not occur.

6. c. The "Temptation Scene" refers to the scene in which Iago tempts and convinces Othello that Desdemona has been unfaithful (III.iii).

7. a. The "Closet Scene" refers to the scene between Hamlet and Gertrude in her bedroom when he seems to be on the point of killing her (III.iv).

8. g. Athens is the setting for *Timon of Athens*. It seems to represent a world of law and repression. Timon scorns Athens for its hypocrisy and the fickleness of the inhabitants who reject him; he flees Athens for the natural world outside the city.

9. a. In *Antony and Cleopatra,* Shakespeare was bound by history, but he creates a hot Egyptian world in Alexandria that is both passionate and political.

10. f. Although the first act of *Othello* occurs in Venice, the last four take place on the island of Cyprus, the dividing point between the civilized world of Venice and the barbaric world of the Turks. In a male world, where Desdemona is very much alone, Othello devolves from the heroic general of the Venetians into the savage infidel of the African world.

11. b. Of course *Hamlet* must be set in a northern European location. Drawing upon the *Historia Danica* by Saxo-Grammaticus, Shakespeare exploits the coldness and barrenness of the countryside—the watch shivering on the battlements, Poles marching on the ice, Ophelia drowning in the creek—all contributing to an atmosphere in a world that is devoid of warmth or love.

12. e. Messina, a city and port in northern Sicily, is the setting for *Much Ado About Nothing,* as it was the setting also for one of Shakespeare's sources, the *Nouvelle* of Matteo Bandello. Appropriately for the comedy, the men are returning from a rather inconsequential war, apparently fomented by Don John, and thus not to be mistaken for any recognizable conflict.

13. c. Shakespeare's Rome in *Julius Caesar* is a city of intrigue, nightly meetings of conspirators, and an easily manipulated public.

14. d. Scotland is the bleak northern setting for *Macbeth*, providing witches and apparitions and a feudal culture for Macbeth's murderous behavior.

15. h. Drawing upon Homer, Chaucer, and others, Shakespeare places the doomed love affair in *Troilus and Cressida*, in Troy, just before the end of the Trojan War.

16. f. In *Othello,* Desdemona is described thus by her father, Brabantio (I.iii.94–96).

17. g. Ophelia recalls Hamlet before his madness (III.i.158–61).

18. e. The grieving Lear weeps over Cordelia's body (V.iii.272–73).

19. j. Othello is remembered by Lodovico (IV.i.275–78).

20. d. Cleopatra is described by Enobarbus, Antony's soldier (II.ii.202–6).

21. b. In *Julius Caesar,* Mark Antony eulogizes Brutus (V.v. 68, 73–75).

22. c. Cassio is described by Iago in *Othello* (I.i.20–24).

23. h. Lear is scorned by his daughter Regan (I.i.296–97).

24. a. Antony is depicted thus by Cleopatra (V.ii.82–86).

25. i. Caithness, a Scotch noble, describes how out of control Macbeth has become (V.ii.13–16).

Hamlet

26. b. Marcellus and Bernardo have seen the ghost twice before (I.i.25).

27. c. Hamlet has evidently studied at the University of Wittenberg, a Protestant university in Germany.

28. b. The castle is Elsinore. Inverness is Macbeth's castle in Scotland; Blenheim is the Duke of Marlborough's home in England.

29. a. The Ghost commands Hamlet to avenge his unnatural murder (I.v.25).

30. a. Ophelia returns Hamlet's gifts because Polonius orders her to do so, saying "Lord Hamlet is a prince; out of thy star;/This must not be" (II.ii.141–42).

31. c. This reference is to Shakespeare's contemporary London, where the boys' companies, "an aery of children," had become so popular that the men of fashion were afraid to patronize the common players for fear of being satirized by the authors who wrote for the children. Thus the regular actors saw fit to play on tour.

32. a. Hamlet kills Polonius where he is spying behind the arras in Gertrude's bedroom (III.iv.25).

33. b. Fortinbras's army marching to Poland to fight for a small plot of ground stirs Hamlet's guilt at his inaction.

34. c. Hamlet shows Gertrude pictures of his father and Claudius (III.iv.53–68).

35. c. The flower that Ophelia does not mention is the forget-me-not, but she does mention rosemary, pansies, fennel, columbines, rue, and violets (IV.v.).

36. c. The age of Hamlet when he returns from England is thirty. This is confirmed by the First Gravedigger who states that he has been sexton there, "thirty years" and came to the job on the "very day young Hamlet was born" (V.i.155).

37. b. There is no reference in the text to Ophelia's drinking poison.

38. b. The character remaining at the end of the play to tell Hamlet's story is Horatio, the rational man, who is not "passion's slave" (III.ii.76).

39. b. There are eight characters who die during the play: Polonius, Rosencrantz and Guildenstern, Ophelia, Gertrude, Laertes, Claudius, and Hamlet.

Fill-ins for Hamlet's speech:

40. question/suffer   43. die/end

41. slings/arms   44. heartache/natural

42. troubles/opposing   45. flesh/devoutly

Actors of *Hamlet*

46. i. David Garrick (1717–1779)

47. e. Kenneth Branagh (1960–)

48. c. William Henry West Betty (1791–1874)

49. f. Richard Burbage (1567–1619)

50. h. Edwin Forrest (1806–1872)

51. b. Thomas Betterton (1635–1710)

52. d. Edwin Booth (1833–1893)

53. j. Laurence Olivier (1907–1989)

54. g. Richard Burton (1925–1984)

55. a. John Barrymore (1882–1942)

Hamlet on Film

56. c. Kevin Kline, Nicol Williamson, Mel Gibson, and Ethan Hawke have all appeared in a film of *Hamlet*. Al Pacino has not—yet.

57. b. In Zeffirelli's film, the first scene shows Gertrude in the family vault weeping over her first husband's tomb. The Ghost of Hamlet's father does not appear until later.

58. c. Ethan Hawke, in this version a film student, speaks the lines while walking down the Action aisle of a Blockbuster store.

59. c. Hollywood is represented in Branagh's film by Charlton Heston as the Player King, Jack Lemmon as Marcellus, and Billy Crystal as the First Gravedigger.

60. b. Although Olivier was having a quarrel with the Technicolor people at the time he was planning *Hamlet,* he felt that black-and-white photography had one "big, big advantage. I could use deep focus photography . . . I could create distances between characters, creating an effect of alienation, or of yearning for past pleasure . . . I was able to use the empty spaces for exciting physical action" (*On Acting.* Simon and Schuster. 289–290).

61. b. Kenneth Branagh chose the dress of the mid-nineteenth century.

62. c. In the interest of turning out a two hour film, Olivier cut Rosencrantz and Guildenstern, and Fortinbras.

63. The chronological order for the films is as follows:

> d. Laurence Olivier produced his *Hamlet* in 1948.
> e. Tony Richardson's film with Nicol Williamson was produced in 1969.
> a. The Franco Zeffirelli/Mel Gibson version appeared in 1990.
> b. Kenneth Branagh produced his film in 1996.
> c. Michael Almereyda's film with Ethan Hawke was released in 2000.

64. Here are the Ophelias and their Hamlets.

> 1. Helena Bonham Carter and (b) Mel Gibson
> 2. Jean Simmons and (d) Laurence Olivier
> 3. Julia Stiles and (c) Ethan Hawke
> 4. Kate Winslet and (a) Kenneth Branagh

65. Here are the Claudiuses and their Gertrudes.

    1. Alan Bates and (b) Glenn Close
    2. Antony Hopkins and (d) Judy Parfitt
    3. Derek Jacobi and (a) Julie Christie
    4. Kyle Maclachlin and (e) Diane Venora
    5. Basil Sydney and (c) Eileen Herlie

Othello

66. a. Iago is disgruntled because Othello named Cassio his lieutenant, when he, Iago, had had the support of "three great ones of the city" as well as the experience and seniority necessary for the job (I.i.).

67. c. "Making the beast with two backs" is one of the vulgar expressions Iago uses as he describes to Brabantio the marriage of Desdemona and Othello (I.i.115).

68. b. Iago tells Othello that

> "Good name in man and woman . . . /Is the immediate jewel of their souls/;Who steals my purse steals trash" (III.iii.155–57).

69. a. Although Iago tells Othello that he saw Cassio with the handkerchief and heard Cassio speak of Desdemona while asleep, the one incontrovertible fact he can use is that Desdemona has lied to her father about the courtship of Othello.

70. b. Othello is referring to the palm of Desdemona's hand, "Hot, hot, and moist" (III.iv.39).

71. c. Desdemona learned the Willow Song from her mother's maid, Barbary (IV.iii.26).

72. b. The adjective used to describe Iago throughout the play is *honest*. Although Desdemona is also termed honest several times, Iago is called honest by Othello and Cassio on some sixteen occasions.

73. a. Othello tells Desdemona that the handkerchief was sewn by "A sibyl, that had number'd in the world/The sun to course two hundred compasses" (III.iv.70–71).

74. b. At the end of the play Cassio is left in charge of Cyprus.

75. Iago describes Cassio (II.i.250–51).

76. Othello is speaking of Iago (III.iii.258–60).

77. Iago describes Bianca (IV.i.95–96).

78. Othello compliments Montano (II.iii.191–93).

79. a. False. Othello says: "I fetch my life and being/From men of royal siege" (I.ii.22).

79. b. False. Brabantio declares Desdemona, "A maiden never bold;/Of spirit so still and quiet, that her motion/Blush'd at herself" (I.iii.94–96).

80. c. True. Cassio says: "I have very poor and unhappy brains for drinking" (II.iii.35–36).

80. d. True. Iago tells Cassio to "importune her help to put you in your place again" (II.iii.324).

81. e. True. Desdemona tells Cassio that she would "rather die/Than give thy cause away"(III.iii.27).

81. f. False. Othello speaks of chopping Desdemona into messes, but his first choice is poison (IV.i.217).

82. g. True. Iago tells Roderigo that Othello is going "into Mauritania and takes away with him the fair Desdemona" (IV.ii. 229–30).

82. h. False. Emilia is slain by Iago from behind (V.ii.235).

Othello on Film

83. The 1999 film adaptation of *Othello,* set in an American high school in the South, is entitled *O.* It is directed by Tim Blake Nelson and the cast includes Melchi Phifer as Odin, John Hartnett as Hugo, and Julia Stiles as Desi.

84. Yaphet Kotto is the actor in a film version of *Othello* directed by Liz White, produced from 1962 to 1966, but not screened publicly until 1980. The cast also includes Richard Dixon as Iago and Audrey Dixon as Desdemona.

85. b. Sir Laurence Olivier, in his autobiography, *On Acting* (Simon & Schuster, 1986), made these remarks about his film performance of Othello, which he felt was not as successful as his earlier stage performance.

86. The director was Orson Welles.

87. c. Trevor Nunn is the director of the *Othello* set in the middle of the nineteenth century.

88. b. Oliver Parker chose to open his film with a Venetian gondola and the tragedy mask.

89. c. Welles's opening shows a long funeral procession with the bodies of Othello and Desdemona and then cuts to a shot of Iago in a metal cage, being hoisted on the castle walls.

90. b. John Kani commits suicide with the horn of an animal that has been hanging around his neck through the film.

91. b. Michael MacLiammoir, in Welles's film, has a small nondescript dog, who performs poignantly in the brilliant bathhouse scene.

Here are the Othellos matched with their correct Iagos.

92. Laurence Fishburne and a. Kenneth Branagh

93. John Kani and c. Richard Hadden Haines

94. Laurence Olivier and b. Frank Finlay

95. Orson Welles and d. Michael MacLiammoir

96. Willard White and e. Ian McKellen

King Lear

97. b. The first two lines of the play announce the thematic questions of one person's value over another's. Here, Gloucester surmises that the King preferred Albany to Cornwall. That theme continues with Lear's conclusion that Goneril and Regan are worth more than Cordelia.

98. The question that Lear asks his three daughters is "Which of you shall we say doth love us most?" (I.i.52).

99. c. Cordelia is the daughter who answers, "Nothing," and continues, "I cannot heave/My heart into my mouth" (I.i.93–94). That is, she cannot express her love in flowery words.

100. a. As Gloucester's illegitimate son, Edmund will not inherit from his father and cannot hope for a decent career or marriage.

101. b. The Fool's function is to act as a truth teller, and although he entertains Lear and attempts to cheer him when he is sad, he primarily acts as Lear's conscience, his alter ego, his analyst.

102. b. When Kent is banished he shaves his beard ("I raz'd my likeness," I.iv.4) and also borrows "other accents" in his speech.

103. c. Edgar disguises himself, shedding his identity, to become "Poor Turlygod! Poor Tom!/That's something yet: Edgar I nothing am" (II.iii.20–21).

104. a. In the numbers game the daughters play with Lear, Goneril says she will have no more than fifty of Lear's servants

stay with her; Regan at first says, "If you will come to me—/For now I spy a danger,—I entreat you/To bring but five and twenty" (II.iv.249–51). A few lines later she asks, "What need One?" (II.iv.266).

105. b. Gloucester is blinded by the foot of Cornwall. He says, "Fellows, hold the chair./Upon these eyes of thine I'll set my foot" (III.vii.67–68).

106. Lear curses Goneril and begs Nature to keep her sterile (I.iv.297–99).

107. Edmund declares his loyalty to the forces of Nature (I.ii.1–2).

108. Regan tells Lear that he is old and on the brink of death (II.iv.149–50).

109. Lear asks whether there is any cause in nature that would account for his daughters' cruelty (III.vi.81).

110. Edmund worries that he may be censured for allowing loyalty to Cornwall to take precedence over his "natural" feelings for his brother (III.v.4–5).

111. After the trial scene, Kent personifies Lear as nature as he gazes at him asleep in the hovel (III.vi.104).

112. The Doctor tells Cordelia that sleep is nature's nurse, and Lear is in need of it (IV.iv.12–13).

113. The blind Gloucester grieves over Lear's ruin as a part of nature (IV.vi.137–38).

114. An anonymous Gentleman tells Lear that his daughter Cordelia redeems nature from its universal curse (IV.vi.209–11).

115. In his dying moments Edmund tries to do one good deed, despite his evil nature (V.iii.243–44).

King Lear on Film

116. a. The Stonehenge location was a choice of the Elliott-Olivier team for their film (1984). It is also used at the end of the film.

117. c. In the Kosintsev version (1970) we see beggars and peasants trudging up the road to the castle from all directions, to hear how their future will be decided with the division of the kingdom. They are the "poor naked wretches" whom Lear has not regarded (III.iv.28).

118. d. Kurasawa notes that according to Goneril (I.iii.7) Lear is out hunting, so he presents him in the opening of his film (1985) in the act of shooting.

119. b. Peter Brook was influenced by Jan Kott's essay in his film of 1971 and emphasizes the absurdity of the human condition.

120. d. Kurasawa's film, entitled *Ran* (1985), calls upon an old Japanese legend of three faithful sons. His Lear asserts that three arrows bundled together cannot be broken, but a single arrow can be; the rebellious son, who parallels Cordelia, protests against the division of the kingdom and breaks the bundle apart.

121. a. This is a scene in the Elliott-Olivier film.

122. c. Oleg Dal's anguished "Howl, howl, howl" produces a long echo from the surrounding hills.

123. d. Again in Kurasawa's *Ran,* the character Sue, fleeing with her brother, returns to pick up his beloved flute and is killed.

124. b. At the end of Brook's *Lear,* Paul Scofield looks to the heavens, perhaps to see Cordelia's spirit, and slowly falls out of the frame. The screen goes to white.

125. c. Kosintsev's Fool opens the film playing on his pipe and also ends it weeping as the body of Lear passes.

Macbeth on Film

126. a. Orson Welles produced a stage version of *Macbeth* set on the island of Haiti, since he felt that the force of the supernatural in such a setting would be more credible. His film version (1948) is set in Scotland, but he kept the "voodoo" drums.

127. b. The English title of Kurasawa's adaptation of *Macbeth* (1957) is *Throne of Blood*. In Japanese the title translates as *The Castle of the Spider.*

128. b. The scene described is the opening of Trevor Nunn's *Macbeth* (1978).

129. d. Kurasawa's film has only one witch.

130. a. The witches make a clay effigy of Macbeth with a crown on his head in Orson Welles's film.

131. c. The scene described is the opening of Roman Polanski's film.

132. c. In Polanski's film, we see Macbeth go up the stairs into Duncan's room, where he stares at the sleeping King. Suddenly Duncan awakes, says, "Macbeth!" and Macbeth stabs him. The other films stay with the text, with Lady Macbeth waiting below while the murder occurs.

133. b. Trevor Nunn's film of *Macbeth* occurs on a bare stage with no sets, only a few pieces, so the actors are filmed mostly in close-up. They are in simple unadorned contemporary clothes.

134. c. In Kurasawa's *Throne of Blood,* Macbeth (Washizu) is killed by many arrows, one of which pierces his throat.

Here are the Macbeths with their Lady Macbeths:

135. Jon Finch and a. Francesca Annis

136. Ian McKellen and b. Judi Dench

137. Toshire Mifume and d. Izuzu Yazmada

138. Orson Welles and c. Jeanette Nolan

139. The story goes that Shakespeare included the three witches in *Macbeth* to ingratiate himself with James I, who had written a book on demonology. Apparently, some of the incantations were authentic and angered those who considered them sacred. In retaliation, they cursed the play and its productions evermore. Through the centuries there have been mishaps, accidents, illnesses, and deaths associated with *Macbeth,* and even mentioning the title is considered unlucky.

Antony and Cleopatra

140. a. The play is set in 40 B.C., a watershed in human history; the years just before the birth of Christ, when the Roman republic gave way to the empire, and the world stood on the brink of several hundred years of peace.

141. c. The Caesar in the play is Julius's great-nephew, Octavius, named as heir in Caesar's will.

142. Octavius Caesar (a), Lepidus (b), and Mark Antony are the "triple pillars," a triumvirate formed to avoid civil war between the conflicting powers of Caesar and Antony.

143. c. When Fulvia dies, Antony marries Octavia, Caesar's sister, to cement his shaky relationship with Caesar.

144. b. Iras is Cleopatra's other woman, who succumbs first to the asp's sting, occasioning Cleopatra's lament that if Iras meets Antony first in the other world, he'll "spend that kiss/ Which is my heaven to have" (V.ii.305–306).

145. c. Menas suggests to Pompey that he could cut the cable, and "when we are put off, fall to their throats./All there is thine" (II.vi.76–78). Pompey rejects the idea, saying that Menas should have done it and not talked about it.

146. b. The decisive naval battle is fought at Actium.

147. c. The night before the battle the soldiers hear strange music, and wonder whether it is in the air or the earth, and whether it is a good sign. The Third Soldier replies, "No," and the Second Soldier says, "'Tis the god Hercules, whom Antony lov'd,/Now leaves him" (IV.iii.17–18).

148. b. Antony bungles his suicide and is dying slowly. Told that Cleopatra is alive, he has himself carried to the pyramid and hoisted up to die in her arms.

The verbs that Shakespeare uses in this well-known passage are as follows:

149. h. wither

150. g. stale

151. c. cloy

152. d. feed

153. e. hungry

154. f. satisfies

155. a. become

156. b. bless

157. Laurence Olivier and Vivien Leigh played the title roles in Shakespeare's *Antony and Cleopatra* and alternated in George Bernard Shaw's *Caesar and Cleopatra* in 1951.

Coriolanus

158. c. The basic conflict of the play is between the patricians and the commoners.

159. b. Shakespeare appeared to want a hero whose pride and arrogance would lead to his fall.

160. d. Menenius explains how the various members of the body rebelled against the "cormorant belly" and the belly responded that the foot it digests goes to help the other members function: "I am the store-house and the shop / Of the whole body" (I.i.137–38).

161. e. Menenius Agrippa identifies the First Citizen as "the great toe . . . For that, being one of th' lowest, basest, poorest . . . thou goest foremost" (I.i.160–62).

162. e. Caius Marcius has supreme contempt for the commoners, calling them cowards and curs. But he admires Tullus Aufidius, saying, "He is a lion / That I am proud to hunt" (I.i.239–40). These sentiments do not endear him to the populace.

163. b. Volumnia loves Caius Marcius because he is a brave warrior and she can live vicariously through him. She says, "Had I a dozen sons . . . I had rather have eleven die nobly for their country / Than one voluptuously surfeit out of action" (I.iii.24–27).

164. a. Although Marcius does all the things mentioned, the act of entering the city of Corioli alone and taking it earns him the title of Coriolanus. The Herald announces:

"Know, Rome, that all alone Marcius did fight
Within Corioles gates: where he hath won,
With fame, a name to Caius Marcius; these
In honour follows Coriolanus." (II.i.179–82)

165. f. Sicinius turns the citizens of Rome against Corio-

lanus by emphasizing his contempt for them (a), and by urging them to exercise the power that they have (d).

166. a. When Coriolanus loses his temper before the plebians, they demand that he be banished as a traitor (III.iii.94–108).

167.c. Infuriated, Coriolanus banishes the city with a speech that begins

"You common cry of curs! whose breath I hate
As reek of the rotten fens, whose loves I prize
As the dead carcasses of unburied men
That do corrupt my air, I banish you!" (III.iii.120–23)

168. b. Coriolanus travels to Antium, to the house of Aufidius, where he offers his throat and/or his service (IV.v.71–107).

169. b. The pleadings of Volumnia serve to sway Coriolanus from destroying Rome, which permits Aufidius to call him traitor and hired assassins to kill him.

Timon of Athens

170 a. The play is a satiric essay on the pervasiveness of greed and the corrupting power of money, demonstrated by the friends from various professions who sponge from Timon.

171. b. Perhaps he has a soft spot in his heart for everyone, as Timon cannot help giving money to make others more comfortable, to support their talents, to relieve their debts.

172. a. Although Flavius tries to restrain him, Timon pays for his gifts through loans he has made.

173. c. Apemantus says, "I'll nothing: for if I should be bribed too, there would be none left to rail upon thee, and then thou wouldst sin the faster" (I.ii.244–246).

174. c. None of Timon's friends refers to the stars as an excuse for their ungenerous behavior. Lucullus (a) says, "This is no time to lend money, especially upon bare friendship, without security" (III.i.42–43). Lucius (b) at first thinks that Timon's request is a joke, and then regrets that he spent so much the day before (III.ii.51). Sempronius (d) claims to be hurt that he is the last one to be asked (III.iii.11).

175 b. Alcibiades appeals to the senate to save a friend's life who has committed murder. The senate rejects his appeal and banishes Alcibiades (III.v.).

176. c. At the banquet, Timon dumps the water in the faces of his guests, and then throws them out with the dinner dishes (III.vi.).

177. c. Timon takes up residence in a cave by the sea.

178. b. Disgusted with humanity, Timon leaves Athens because in the woods he will find "Th' unkindest beast more kinder than mankind" (IV.i.36).

179. b. "Earth," says Timon, digging the ground, "Yield me roots!" (IV.iii.22).

180. c. Timon recognizes that Flavius is his one true friend; when Flavius says, "Oh, let me stay/And comfort you" (IV.iii.540–541) Timon gives him gold and tells him not to come back.

181. c. The senators want Timon to return to Athens "to take the captainship . . . Allow'd with absolute power . . . so soon we shall drive back/Of Alcibiades the approaches wild" (V.i.164– 67).

Heroines and Hamlets

182. a. Dame Judith Anderson (1898–1992)

183. b. Dame Peggy Ashcroft (1907–1991)

184. d. Sarah Bernhardt (1844–1923)

185. f. Dame Judi Dench (1934–)

186. l. Sarah Siddons (1755–1831)

187. c. Charlotte Barnes (1818–1863)

188. e. Charlotte Cushman (1816–1876)

189. j. Fanny Kemble (1809–1893)

190. k. Hannah Pritchard (1711–1768)

191. n. Dame Sybil Thorndike (1882–1976)

192. m. Ellen Terry (1847–1928)

193. i. Uta Hagen (1919–)

194. g. Colleen Dewhurst (1924–1991)

195. h. Eleanora Duse (1858–1924)

ACT V

Superstars

Superstars are those who know or think they know just about everything about Shakespeare. Still, amateurs, apprentices, professionals, and major players should not be intimidated. It's true, Superstars have studied the plays religiously, have seen productions such as *1, 2,* and *3 Henry VI* (which are not included here) and maybe even the bad quarto of *Hamlet* (also not included here). They are awesomely erudite and enthusiastic, and so dedicated that they would never dream of leaving a dreadful production of *Measure for Measure* at the intermission, and they can even find excuses for the Macbeth who jumps on tables and has hysterics in the banquet scene.

So this section is for them, and the questions are deliberately difficult and concern plays less frequently studied or produced. There are some matching sections, and they are devilish, but the multiple choices are no picnic, either. The superstars will most likely breeze right through them, and could probably suggest a few questions of their own to stump friends who are also superstars. However, you lesser mortals might be surprised that some of your responses are right on target and that you are an unrecognized Superstar yourself.

Shakespeare himself at this point was the seventeenth-

century version of a superstar. He was recognized and respected, his plays were performed frequently, he was able to
wheel and deal in real estate in Stratford-upon-Avon, and write
a play or two in the comfort of his own home there and send it
down to London for production.

Here are questions about his late plays, with a few diver-
sions to tease you. They begin with Sibling Scramble, move to
Pericles, Mistakes and Mishaps, *Cymbeline,* Lovers and Luna-
tics, *The Winter's Tale,* Adjectives, *The Tempest* and *The Two
Noble Kinsmen. Beat the Bard* ends with Bard Buster I and
Bard Buster II, guaranteed to blow your mind.

There are 180 questions, and the answers begin on page 210.

Sibling Scramble

Shakespeare's plays are rich in sibling pairs and multiples,
some who love and care for one another, some who are out for
blood—and who often get it.

Arrange the characters below into their appropriate family
groups, which might be pairs or threesomes. Don't despair;
some are very easy!

Antipholus of	Don Pedro	Viola
Ephesus	Dromio of Ephesus	Katherine
Antipholus of	Dromio of Syracuse	Laertes
Syracuse	Edward IV	Oliver
Antonio	Goneril	Ophelia
Arviragus	Guiderius	Orlando
Bassianus	Hamlet	Paris
Bianca	Hector	Prospero
Clarence	Helenus	Regan
Claudio	Henry, Prince of Wales	Richard III
Cordelia	Imogen	Saturninus
Deiphobus	Isabella	Sebastian
Don John	John of Lancaster	Troilus

1. This is a pair of twins.

   _____

2. This is another pair of twins.

   _____

3. And this is a third pair of twins.

   _____

4. One's a bad apple, and tries to have his brother killed, but converts to a moral life at the end and gets a nice girl.

   _____

5. Another's a bad apple, and usurps his sibling's dukedom, but repents at the end and is forgiven by his sibling.

   _____

6. One's a really bad apple and never converts.

   _____

7. Two are bad apples, but get their just rewards; their sibling meets a tragic end.

   _____

8. One of these three is unknown to the others until the fifth act.

   _____

9. This one needs his sibling's help to save him from execution.

   _____

10. These give their all for a sibling's love for a woman unworthy of him.

    _____

11. This one becomes an emperor, but his sibling gets the girl.

     _____

12. At the beginning one is "curst," and the other is "sweet," but their roles are reversed at the end of the play.

     _____

13. One caused a rebellion against his half sibling, and continues his mischief, even though his brother has forgiven him.

     _____

14. These two young royals fight bravely against the French.

     _____

15. This brother and sister are extremely sad at being parted.

     _____

Perhaps Shakespeare was still experimenting in these late romances. In this, the first of them, all the elements of the genre appear: thrilling adventures of the central figure, action occurring in remote lands, separation and reunion of the family, the miraculous restoration of life after apparent death. He does it better in the later romances, however.

Pericles

16. The home of Prince Pericles is

    a. Tarsus
    b. Tyre
    c. Actium

17. In act 1, Pericles is visiting in Antioch

    a. in hopes, like Petruchio, of wiving it wealthily
    b. as guest of his childhood friend Antiochus
    c. to negotiate a peace settlement over disputed islands in the Adriatic

18. Pericles's trusted adviser is

    a. Antiochus
    b. Enobarbus
    c. Helicanus

19. Antiochus wants to kill Pericles because

    a. Pericles wants to marry his daughter
    b. Pericles interprets the riddle correctly
    c. Pericles challenges him to a duel

20. After fleeing his kingdom on the advice of Helicanus, who urges him to "travel for a while," Pericles journeys to Tarsus, where he gains the gratitude of Cleon and Dionyza by

    a. providing them with ammunition to turn back the neighboring Cretans
    b. providing them with corn as their people are starving
    c. teaching them how to foretell the future by the stars

21. Pericles's good deed in Tarsus is echoed by the fishermen's charity when he is shipwrecked. They provide him with

    a. a fishnet so he can make his own living
    b. food and clothes to warm him
    c. a leaky boat to continue his journey

22. The engagement of Thaisa and Pericles is solemnized

    a. when she says in a letter than she will marry no one else
    b. when Simonides declares that she must marry Pericles or live as a nun the rest of her life
    c. when Pericles announces he will slay anyone who crosses him

23. The way in which Thaisa supposedly dies is

    a. in childbirth
    b. by being swept overboard in a great storm
    c. by being captured by pirates

24. Pericles buries Thaisa at sea because

    a. the chest she has been placed in is swept overboard in the storm
    b. the god Apollo appears in a streak of lightning and tells him to do it
    c. the sailors believe the storm will not stop until the ship is cleared of the dead

25. Antiochus and his daughter die in spectacular fashion

    a. by their own hands
    b. in a tremendous storm
    c. in a fire from heaven

26. The number of years that elapse while Pericles roams the seas is approximately

    a. five
    b. ten
    c. sixteen

27. After the supposed deaths of Thaisa and Marina, Pericles vows

    a. never to cut his hair
    b. to eat only bread and water
    c. to remain celibate

28. The evil Dionyza hires Leonine to kill Marina because

    a. she thinks Marina is a nasty little brat
    b. Marina outdoes Dionyza's daughter in every way
    c. Marina is planning to run away with one of the palace guards

29. Captured by pirates and sold to a brothel, Marina maintains her virginity by

    a. converting her clients to moral behavior
    b. bribing her clients
    c. threatening them with naming names to the authorities

30. Marina manages to escape the brothel by

    a. buying her way out with gold from Lysimachus, the governor
    b. convincing the bawd that she is ill with a communicable disease
    c. finding a better job as a chef

31. Pericles does not believe he has found his daughter until she tells him

    a. her name
    b. she is a king's daughter
    c. she was born at sea

    d. Cleon and his wife tried to murder her
    e. the good palace guard helped her escape
    f. she was captured by pirates
    g. she is the daughter of King Pericles
    h. all of the above
    i. all of the above except e

32. The goddess that Thaisa dedicates herself to is

    a. Venus
    b. Diana
    c. Proserpina

33. When the people of Tarsus learn of the deeds of the wicked Cleon and Dionyza, they

    a. decapitate them and place their heads on pikes
    b. exile them to the desert with little food or water
    c. burn them up in their palace

34. This is a play about fathers and daughters. Match the parent and child below:

    a. No-Name Daughter   c. Philoten
    b. Marina   d. Thaisa

    1. Antiochus _____
    2. Cleon _____
    3. Pericles _____
    4. Simonides _____

Mistakes and Mishaps

Here's a diversion. In a number of Shakespeare's plays, the action turns on an accident or mistake. These may give you a

little trouble, but on the other hand, only one question is from
a play that has not appeared yet. Identify the play and players
who are involved in such events.

35. A jeweler gives a golden chain to the wrong person, and
    the person who was supposed to get it berates the jeweler
    for not giving it to him, as his wife expects it.

    _____   _____

36. A servant can't read, so the invitation list must be read to
    him, an act that results in several young men crashing the
    party.

    _____   _____

37. A handkerchief is dropped, and its peregrinations
    afterward lead to tragedy.

    _____   _____

38. A person eavesdropping behind the arras is mistakenly
    killed.

    _____   _____

39. A prisoner fortuitously dies of natural causes, and his
    head is substituted for that of another.

    _____   _____

40. A servant overhears a conversation in the garden and
    mistakes its contents.

    _____   _____

41. A servant mistakes one Athenian for another.

    _____   _____

42. A spirited horse rears up and throws his rider, who luckily dies to resolve the action of the play.

   _____   _____

43. A sleeping man, a snake wrapped around his neck, is stalked by a lioness. The man's estranged brother comes upon him unexpectedly and saves him from probable death. The brothers are reconciled.

   _____   _____

Cymbeline

Cymbeline is a play that was overlooked for many years; however, the twenty-first century is demonstrating a renewed interest in its romantic and complicated plot, and productions have been mounted in New York, Stratford-upon-Avon, and elsewhere. The questions that follow may encourage you to seek out a production in your own area.

44. Posthumus Leonatus was so-named because of a peculiar

   a. birthmark resembling a lion's head
   b. occurrence in nature the moment of his birth
   c. circumstance regarding his father.

45. King Cymbeline had two sons twenty years earlier but they

   a. died in a hunting accident
   b. were stolen from him by an angry retainer
   c. were deformed and so were put aside because of the shame of their condition.

46. Though raised at court, Posthumus is banished from the King's presence because

   a. he longs to have the place held by Cloten, the Queen's son
   b. he irritated Cloten to the breaking point
   c. he is indiscreet enough to fall in love with the King's daughter

47. Love tokens are exchanged between

   a. Imogen and Posthumus
   b. Posthumus and the Queen
   c. Cloten and Posthumus—their little secret, reminiscent of the friendship between Shakespeare and the Earl of Southampton, the "handsome young man" of the sonnets

48. In Rome, Posthumus exhibits bad taste by

   a. betting his love token on his beloved's fidelity
   b. angering his host by engaging in a heated argument with another guest
   c. mocking the exaggerations of the Italian Lothario who would ultimately convince him of his wife's infidelity

49. The Queen asks the doctor, Cornelius, to provide her with

   a. a box of poisons
   b. a box of cordials
   c. a collection of flowers gathered while the dew was still on the ground

50. The doctor provides her with

    a. a box of poisons
    b. a box of sedatives
    c. medicine for the King's impotence

51. Iachimo's first attempt to seduce Imogen

    a. fails, but he turns the experience into an advantage by revealing that the seduction was a test, which she passed with flying colors
    b. fails, upon which she calls Pisanio to carry Iachimo to the King and reveal his treachery
    c. fails, and he decides that he cannot win the wager

52. When Iachimo climbs out of the trunk placed in Imogen's bedroom for safe-keeping, he

    a. takes note of her chamber's appointments, the moles on her body, and the book she is reading
    b. steals the bracelet, a love token given to Imogen by Posthumus
    c. almost kisses her lips as she sleeps
    d. has enough evidence of a seduction without actually seducing her
    e. all of the above

53. Cloten tries to seduce Imogen by having

    a. musicians sing an aubade, or morning song, to her
    b. bouquets of flowers sent to her at regular intervals
    c. gifts of candies, sweetmeats, and precious ices sent to her bedchamber

54. Imogen's response to Cloten's approaches stimulates him to find and wear a suit of clothing that belonged to

    a. Posthumus
    b. Alexander the Great
    c. Julius Caesar

55. Posthumus's misogynistic outcry, in which he rejects all women including his mother, is

    a. a result of Imogen's fidelity and ability to see through Iachimo's treachery
    b. a result of the evil trickery of Iachimo
    c. the summary action of his betting ill-advisedly his love token from Imogen

56. In Wales, near Milford-Haven, Imogen, disguised as a boy named Fidele,

    a. accepts the hospitality of Morgan and his two sons
    b. meets and rejects again Cloten, who has followed her to Milford-Haven
    c. appears to be dead, causing the two sons of Morgan, Polydore and Cadwal, to sing (or recite) a beautiful mourning song
    d. finds Cloten's severed head and flings it rudely into the river
    e. *a* and *c* but not *b* and *d*
    f. *b* and *c* but not *a* and *d*

57. Cadwal and Polydore, Morgan's adopted sons, are really

    a. Arviragus and Guiderius, Cymbeline's lost sons
    b. Cadwal and Polydore, Cloten's long-lost brothers stolen from the Queen twenty years before she met and fell in love with Cymbeline

    c. Belarius's real sons whom he has protected all these years by suggesting that they were left at his doorstep—he left the court to protect them from the jealous rages of Cymbeline

58. In a deathlike swoon, Imogen is buried in a cave; she awakens next to

    a. a headless male whom she believes is Posthumus
    b. a headless male whom she believes is Cloten
    c. a headless male who turns out to be Iachimo
    d. a headless male who turns out to be Pisanio, the loyal retainer of Posthumus, who followed Imogen to Milford-Haven to protect her

59. When Posthumus appears in the garb of a soldier, he is fighting for

    a. the Britons
    b. the Romans
    c. the Welsh

60. He realizes that he is

    a. fighting for the wrong side
    b. fighting for the right side
    c. fighting for the love of battle—"O God, I love it so . . ."
    d. fighting to please Mars, the god of war

61. The function of the dream sequence employing Posthumus's mother, father, and Jupiter is

    a. to show that the prophecy of Posthumus's greatness is fulfilled
    b. to restore Posthumus to health, wealth, and happiness at court with Imogen

c. to reveal the divine concern that has hovered over Posthumus through thick and thin, good and bad, since his unusual birth

d. all of the above

62. The Queen dies

    a. loving Cymbeline
    b. hating Cymbeline
    c. loving Imogen
    d. hating Imogen
    e. in despair
    f. *a*, *c*, and *e*
    g. *b*, *d*, and *e*

63. Posthumus strikes Imogen down

    a. by mistake, thinking her to be an interfering page boy
    b. in anger as a result of Iachimo's confession
    c. to prove to Pisanio that Posthumus's commands should be obeyed without question
    d. when she defends Guiderius for slaying Cloten at Milford-Haven

64. Iachimo yields up to Posthumus the ring offered as payment for the wager as well as

    a. the bracelet stolen from Imogen
    b. the box of cordials left behind by Imogen in the cave in Milford-Haven
    d. the pardon given him by Posthumus, which becomes the theme of the denouement: "Pardon's the word to all"

65. In the final scene

    a. Cymbeline is reunited with his lost sons
    b. Cymbeline is reunited with his lost sons and daughter
    c. Cymbeline is reunited with his lost sons, daughter, and
       son-in-law

66. Identify the character or characters who require pardon
    for their actions at the end of the play:

    a. Posthumus for his abuse of Iachimo
    b. Iachimo for his abuse of Posthumus
    c. Cymbeline for his treatment of the Queen
    d. Cymbeline for his treatment of Cloten
    e. Guiderius for his beheading of Cloten
    f. Morgan (Belarius) for raising the King's sons poorly
    g. Imogen for pursuing her husband to Milford-Haven
    h. all of the above except *c*

Did you get caught on this one?

Lovers and Lunatics

Shakespeare's plays abound with lovers and lunatics (those
who pursue unwilling or inappropriate choices). Here are some
of them and their various methods of pursuit. Name these eager
romantics.

67. I steal some of my father's money and the turquoise ring
    my mother gave him, dress myself as a boy, and run off
    with my lover.

    _____

68. The lady I love has been shut up by her father because
    she is not interested in the rich man her father wants her

to marry, so I make a rope ladder to rescue her. Unfortunately, my best friend betrays me, her father catches me, and I am banished.

_____

69. I have given my friend jewels "that would half have corrupted a votarist" to win me acquaintance with the woman I desire. Her father has said he would rather I'd had her than her present husband, and my friend keeps telling me she'll get tired of her choice and welcome my solicitation, but so far I've gotten nowhere.

_____

70. Like the fellow above, I have a friend who has supported my suit to his niece and taken my money. She has vowed to mourn for seven years, so I'm not too encouraged, but meanwhile we have a rousing good time, singing, drinking, and playing tricks on the Puritan.

_____

71. I make my move on the woman I desire when she is following the funeral procession of her father-in-law, whom I murdered. At first she spits at me, but I am so persuasive, that eventually she accepts my ring.

_____

72. I woo the lady to win a wager about her fidelity; when she doesn't believe my lies about her husband, I resort to trickery, hiding in a chest delivered to her room and stealing a bracelet from her arm as she sleeps.

_____

73. It is love at first sight for me—I'm almost sure she is a goddess. But her harsh father insists upon testing me and

my love. He makes me carry "Some thousands of these logs and pile them up," but I really don't mind because she "makes my labours pleasures."

74. My love is so much above me in status that he will not even look at me, the daughter of a doctor. When the King rewards me for curing his illness by providing my love as a husband, he rejects me and runs off. I have to resort to the bed trick to win him.

75. In the midst of my assignation with this merry wife, I learn that her husband is about to arrive with all the officers of Windsor. I manage to escape detection by jumping into the dirty laundry basket, but unfortunately end up in a muddy ditch.

76. I loved the sight of her when I came back from the war, and I had no problem becoming engaged, because the Duke wooed her for me. But a friend tells me that she is false, and I think I see her at her window talking to another man, so I reject her at the altar.

77. My love is so lovesick that I tell him that I will cure his condition if he will pretend that I am his love and woo me. Since I am dressed as a boy he doesn't recognize me and is willing to play the game. I tease him and tell him that he doesn't even look or dress like a lover.

78. I love the apparent daughter of a shepherd; when my father, the King, finds out, he tries to break us up, but with

the help of an old lord we flee to Sicilia and eventually win his approval.

_____

79. My love was so intense and so romantic that my name has become synonymous with lover. I was rash and impulsive; our families had been feuding for centuries, so there was nothing but a tragic end awaiting us.

_____

80. I courted the beautiful daughter of a Venetian senator. She could have had any aristocratic young lord in Venice, and I was honored when she chose me. In fact, I wondered somewhat why she had. Perhaps that is one reason I was so easily gulled into believing she was unfaithful.

_____

81. My friends and I took a vow to study for three years and not become involved with women. But when the Princess comes with her ladies, we all forget our vow (although I am the last to do so), and pursue our ladies with enthusiasm.

_____

The Winter's Tale

A bittersweet story of separation and reunion, this play enjoys frequent productions.

82. The amount of time that passes between the first three acts of the play, with its overtones of tragedy, and the last two acts, which burst with comedy, is

   a. ten years
   b. sixteen years
   c. six months

83. The first act of the play takes place in

   a. Sicilia
   b. Bohemia
   c. Romania

84. Polixenes, king of Bohemia, has been a houseguest at
   Leontes' palace for a period of

   a. two weeks
   b. one month
   c. nine months, but who's counting?

85. Leontes accuses his wife, Hermione, of

   a. spending too much money on clothes for Mamillius
   b. carrying Polixenes' child
   c. flirting brazenly with Antigonus

86. When Leontes details Hermione's supposed crimes to
   Camillo, and engages Camillo to do away with Polixenes,

   a. Camillo defends Hermione, then agrees to poison
      Polixenes
   b. Camillo defends Hermione, and refuses to kill
      Polixenes
   c. Camillo agrees with Leontes that Hermione is a
      "bed-swerver" and agrees to kill Polixenes

87. When Hermione gives birth in prison,

   a. Leontes orders that the baby be abandoned in some
      "deserted place"
   b. Leontes orders that the baby be "consum'd with fire"
   c. Leontes orders that the baby be "smothered" in its bed
   d. all of the above

e. *a* and *b* but not *c*
f. *a* and *c* but not *b*

88. After the message from the Oracle is read,

    a. Leontes recognizes he's been wrong
    b. Paulina says the Queen is dead
    c. the Prince Mamillius is dead
    d. all of the above

89. The function of Paulina in the second half of the play is

    a. to raise Perdita
    b. to act as a conscience for Leontes
    c. to take dainties to Hermione in her seclusion

90. Antigonus's fate is to be

    a. eaten by a bear
    b. banished to Romania
    c. imprisoned by Leontes in Sicilia

91. The specific prop called for in the text that Time, the Chorus, enters with is

    a. a scythe
    b. an hourglass
    c. a black hood

92. Polixenes is annoyed with Florizel because

    a. Florizel has been neglecting his princely duties
    b. Florizel has been hanging around the house of a "homely shepherd"
    c. Florizel has been disrespectful to his mother

93. One of the important motifs of this play is

   a. the passage of time
   b. the difficulty of raising children
   c. the need for tolerance

94. Autolycus says he is selling all but

   a. silks and threads
   b. snuffboxes
   c. bracelets and necklaces
   d. ballads

95. In the "Sheep-shearing Scene," Perdita and Polixenes have a pleasant difference of opinion over the qualities of

   a. fortune and nature
   b. art and nature
   c. justice and mercy

96. Seeking refuge from Polixenes' wrath, Florizel and Perdita flee to Sicilia, and tell Leontes that

   a. Polixenes is ill, but sends a friendly greeting
   b. Polixenes is raising a navy to invade Sicilia
   c. Polixenes will never forgive Leontes for his plan to murder him

97. True or False: At the end of the play

   a. Mamillius is restored to life   _____
   b. Perdita marries Florizel   _____
   c. Hermione divorces Leontes   _____
   d. Polixenes and Leontes reconcile   _____
   e. Paulina marries Camillo   _____

98. Considering the meter of the passage below, choose the
    appropriate flower for each blank:

    a. cowslips   d. marjoram
    b. lavender   e. savory
    c. marigold   f. violets

> Here's flow'rs for you;
> Hot (1) _____ , mints, (2) _____ , (3) _____ ,
> The (4) _____ , that goes to bed with th' sun
> And with him rises weeping. (IV.iv.103–106)

Adjectives

Adjectives, they teach us in school, serve to modify nouns in some way, such as to denote a quality, to indicate its quantity, or to distinguish one object from another. After that first lesson, we generally throw adjectives around with abandon, expecting brilliance to result. Unlike us, Shakespeare used adjectives sparingly and purposefully.

Supply the missing adjectives in the quotations below, some of which are easy. If the specific adjective does not come to mind, at the least, marvel at the man's linguistic abilities when you ogle the answers. Whatever else, have fun with this.

99. "Now is the winter of our discontent
    Made _____ summer by this son of York."

100. "O what a rogue and _____ slave am I."

101.   "She never told her love,
    But let concealment, like a worm i' th'bud,
    Feed on her _____ cheek."

102.   "Yet I'll not shed her blood,
    Nor scar that _____ skin of hers than snow,
    And smooth as _____ alabaster."

103. "From forth the _____ loins of these two foes
    A pair of _____ lovers take their life."

104.   "Present fears
    Are less than _____ imaginings."

105. "As flies to _____ boys are we to the gods,
    They kill us for their sport."

106. "I am a very _____, fond old man."

107. "Age cannot wither her, nor custom stale
    Her _____ variety."

108.   "O _____ , _____ world,
    That has such people in't!"

Now Superstars, here is a passage with which the Bard will probably beat you. Try, just try, to supply the adjectives in this magnificent description of Falstaff: (Score 1 for each correct answer.)

109.–116. "There is a devil haunts thee in the likeness of an
        old fat man; a tun of man is thy companion. Why
        dost thou converse with that trunk of humours, that
        (109) _____ of beastliness, that (110) _____
        parcel of dropsies, that (111) _____ bombard
        of sack, that (112) _____ cloak-bag of guts,
        that (113) _____ Manningtree ox with the
        pudding in his belly, that (114) _____ vice,
        that (115) _____ iniquity, that (116) _____
        ruffian, that vanity in years?"

117. Finish off the section with an easy one:
"Thus far, with _____ and all-_____ pen,
Our _____ author hath pursu'd the story."

The Tempest

The Tempest is lovely play of a magical, idealized world.

118. Prospero is on the island because

    a. he is fleeing the police
    b. he wanted a place to retire
    c. his brother usurped his dukedom

119. The lord who provided Prospero with clothes and food so
that he and Miranda could survive the voyage from
Milan in a leaky boat was

    a. Alonso
    b. Gonzalo
    c. Antonio

120. The witch Sycorax confined Ariel in a cloven pine for a
dozen years because

    a. Ariel tried to kill Sycorax with a heavy log
    b. With his magic powers Ariel built a raft and tried to
make an escape from the island
    c. Ariel refused to act on her commands, which were
of a gross nature

121. Prospero promises that if Ariel performs satisfactorily, Ariel will be free

   a. before the day is out
   b. before the next dawn
   c. after two days

Ariel says that he has dispersed the shipwrecked voyagers from Tunis "in troops . . . about the isle." Group the characters below into their appropriate slots:

   a. Adrian   f. Gonzalo
   b. Alonzo   g. Sebastian
   c. Antonio   h. Stephano
   d. Ferdinand   i. Trinculo
   e. Francisco

122. I. _____

123. II. _____

124. III. _____

125. Prospero enslaved Caliban because

   a. he crept into their living quarters one night to steal Prospero's magic book
   b. he crept into their living quarters and tried to rape Miranda
   c. he was very clever at stealing their food

126. The task that Prospero sets for Ferdinand is

    a. to cook a dinner that includes scamels from the
       rocks sautéed in sherry
    b. to pile up logs
    c. to build a fence and paint it white

127. Stephano is saved from drowning by

    a. riding to shore on a butt of sack
    b. riding to shore on the back of a friendly dolphin
    c. grabbing the last lifeboat

128. The plot of Sebastian and Antonio to murder the King of
    Naples is foiled by

    a. Prospero, who catches them just as they are about
       to strike the King and immobilizes them
    b. the King himself, who wakes up after a bee stings
       him
    c. Ariel, who sings a song in his ear

129. Caliban's plot to kill Prospero and make Stephano lord of
    the island can be accomplished, he says, by first

    a. possessing Prospero's books
    b. drugging Prospero's posset
    c. kidnapping Miranda

130. The function of the masque in act 4, scene 1 is

    a. to permit the lovers to enjoy each other's company
       and to learn about each other
    b. to warn the lovers of the many pitfalls of marriage
    c. to celebrate the lovers' virtue and to bless their
       marriage

131. The "glistering apparel" that Ariel brings from Prospero's house in act 4 is

    a. to dress Prospero for his meeting with Alonso and the others
    b. to present to Miranda for her wedding
    c. to lure Stephano and Trinculo into a trap

True or False: At the end of the play

132. Caliban remains unrepentant. _____

133. Miranda will marry Ferdinand. _____

134. Prospero will remain on the island. _____

135. Ariel is freed. _____

136. Prospero banishes Antonio. _____

137. Of the statements below, one has *not* been expressed by a Shakespearean scholar:

    a. "*The Tempest* is a pastoral drama; it is concerned with the opposition of Nature and Art."
    b. *The Tempest* serves as "a mirror powerfully reflecting contemporary concerns, be they social, political, scientific, or moral."
    c. "*The Tempest* is a moral romance, that reminds us of the ambiguous qualities of art and nature, love and illusion, power and politics."
    d. "*The Tempest* is informed throughout by conspiratorial psychology. In seemingly conservative fashion the play appears to reflect and even endorse official discourse in that its action originates within a context of successful conspiracy."

The Two Noble Kinsmen

The Two Noble Kinsmen has not been a great favorite, although it was part of the 2002 Stratford Ontario Shakespeare Festival, and there have been productions throughout the twentieth century. So, interest remains, in this, one of the last of Shakespeare's works.

138. Shakespeare, now apparently retired in Stratford-upon-Avon, had a collaborator for this play named

    a. John Fletcher
    b. John Webster
    c. John Ford

139. The two dramatists are indebted to at least two of the following for the plots (come on, Superstars, you can figure this out). The one who was *not* a source was

    a. Boccaccio
    b. Chaucer
    c. Ovid

140. The noble kinsmen, Palamon and Arcite, are

    a. brothers
    b. cousins
    c. friends

141. In act 1, scene 1, the Three Queens have the audacity to interrupt Theseus's wedding ceremony to beg him

    a. to spare the lives of their sons, who have been captured and sentenced to execution
    b. to recover their husbands' bodies, which are lying on the battlefield rotting in gross fashion
    c, to restore their rightful lands, which Theseus has grabbed

142. Palamon and Arcite are determined to leave Thebes because

    a. Creon is a tyrant, and they don't like his methods
    b. they're bored with their lives in Thebes and there are no girls
    c. they want to find some battle where they can prove their nobility

143. In prison, the ideal of a perfect friendship is expressed by Palamon and Arcite until

    a. Palamon is offered to a release by King Theseus
    b. Arcite escapes through the window with a bedsheet and the help of Emilia
    c. they both see Emilia in the garden

144. The Jailer's Daughter is betrayed by

    a. Palamon, who promises love and then rejects her
    b. Arcite, who promises to take her away from her oafish wooer, but doesn't
    c. her own fantasies about Palamon's attentions

145. When Palamon and Arcite meet in the forest after Palamon has escaped from the jail with the help of the Jailer's Daughter and Arcite has been released by Theseus, they decide to

    a. fight to the death for the love of Emilia
    b. forget the girl and return to Thebes while the going is good
    c. set up a ménage à trois

146. Before the duel, Arcite prays to Mars for military skill. The reply he receives is

     a. "Beware the left hand of your opponent"
     b. a great clanging of armor and sounds of battle
     c. "Get the woman's love first"

147. Before the duel, Palamon prays to Venus, asking for a sign. The reply he receives is

     a. a burst of multicolored fireworks over his head
     b. "Venus smiles not on a battlefield."
     c. sounds of music and the fluttering of doves' wings

148. c. At the end of the play, the Jailor's Daughter

     a. drowns like Ophelia in the rushing brook
     b. goes off to the city to find a new love
     c. will marry the Wooer

149. At the end of the play, Emilia is

     a. won by Palamon
     b. won by Arcite
     c. dead

150. The theme of this play might be expressed as

     a. to the victor go the spoils
     b. justice and forgiveness
     c. innocence and experience

Bard Buster I

Here is a quiz that was given to undergraduate students at a university sometime back in the sixties. Superstars who know a bit about the Elizabethan theater, should have no trouble with it.

Match the description with the items in the key below. (Note: there are four extra.)

a. Addenbrooke, John
b. Alleyn, Edward
c. Arden, Mary
d. Armin, Robert
e. Burbage, Richard
f. *Cardenio*
g. Davenant, Sir William
h. Greene, Robert
i. Griffin, Bartholomew
j. *Groatsworth of Wit*
k. Hall, John
l. Hathaway, Anne
m. Henslowe, Philip
n. *Law Against Lovers*
o. Lucy, Sir Thomas
p. Manningham, John
q. Marston, John
r. Meres, Francis
s. Oxford, Earl of
t. Pembroke, Earl of
u. *The Puritan Widow*
v. Rowe, Nicholas
w. Collins, Francis
x. Kempe, Will

151. The author of *A Groatsworth of Wit*   _____

152. Man from whom Shakespeare is rumored to have stolen a deer   _____

153. Shakespeare's son-in-law, a physician   _____

154. William Pembroke   _____

155. Comedian of Shakespeare's company before 1599

156. Play by Sir William Davenant based on *Measure for Measure*   _____

157. The principal tragedian of Shakespeare's
company   _____

158. Keeper of a diary and financier of the
Lord Admiral's company   _____

159. Law student who kept a commonplace book
with anecdotes about Shakespeare   _____

160. Shakespeare's mother's maiden name _____

161. Lost play, possibly by Shakespeare and
Fletcher   _____

162. Overseer and witness to Shakespeare's
will   _____

163. Edward de Vere   _____

164. Work containing the earliest allusion to
Shakespeare's activity in London   _____

165. Playwright rumored to be Shakespeare's
illegitimate son   _____

166. Comedian of Shakespeare's company
after 1599   _____

167. First biographer of Shakespeare   _____

168. Author of *Palladis Tamia*   _____

169. Play included in the Third Folio but
probably not by Shakespeare   _____

170. Shakespeare's wife   _____

And finally, here is a potpourri of trivia related to the plays, to Shakespeare, and to other vaguely interesting things, that only the most erudite people in the universe will be able to answer correctly. But you might find the answers interesting.

Bard Buster II

171. Name the play, other than *Romeo and Juliet,* in which the hero flees to Mantua.

172. There are seven women who masquerade as men in various plays. They are

    a. _____

    b. _____

    c. _____

    d. _____

    e. _____

    f. _____

    g. _____

173. The American who spearheaded the restoration of the Globe is

    _____

174. What is the significance of these dates?

    a. January 6 _____
    b. March 15 _____
    c. two weeks before Lammastide, August 1 _____
    d. June 21–24 _____
    e. October 25 _____

175. Which one of the following roles did Shakespeare surely *not* play?

    a. Hamlet's Ghost
    b. Adam in *As You Like It*
    c. Richard in *Richard III*

176. Name the actor whose chief claim to fame is having played Othello over three thousand times—in Armenian, Russian, Italian, and French.

    _____

177. In *Ran,* a Japanese version of *King Lear,* Kurosawa makes a major change in the dramatis personae to accommodate the culture of ancient Japan. What is that change?

    _____

178. Adaptations of Shakespeare's plays appeared during the Restoration and eighteenth century under strange names. Identify the plays that appeared under these titles:

    a. *Sauny the Scot* _____
    b. *The History and Fall of
       Caius Marcius* _____
    c. *The Enchanted Island* _____
    d. *Love Betrayed; or
       The Agreeable Disappointment* _____
    e. *The Injured Princess* _____
    f. *The Universal Passion* _____
    g. *Love in a Forest* _____

179. This actor, who called himself a count, was so bad playing Hamlet that the audience regularly pelted him with vegetables. In order to defend himself he was obliged to erect a huge net across the front of the stage.

    _____

180. Name the gentleman, of moderate wealth, whose goal of introducing all the birds that Shakespeare mentioned in his plays led him to release eighty imported European starlings in New York's Central Park on March 16, 1890.

_____

Maybe those weren't fair. Maybe you didn't know any of the answers. But who told you that it was easy to Beat the Bard?

Answers

Sibling Scramble

1. The first pair of twins is Antipholus of Ephesus and Antipholus of Syracuse, who appear in *A Comedy of Errors.*

2. The second pair of twins is Dromio of Ephesus and Dromio of Syracuse, who also appear in *A Comedy of Errors.*

3. The third twins are Viola and Sebastian, shipwrecked in Illyria in *Twelfth Night.*

4. In *As You Like It,* Oliver's hatred of his brother Orlando dissolves when Orlando saves him from the lioness and he wins the love of Celia.

5. Prospero's brother, Antonio, usurps his dukedom and exiles Prospero to a remote island in *The Tempest.* But when he is shipwrecked, Antonio is reconciled to his brother, and they return to Milan peacefully.

6. Richard III is a really bad apple, but his brothers, Clarence and Edward IV, are not much better. Richard never converts. These three brothers appear in *3 Henry VI* and in *Richard III.*

7. Goneril and Regan in *King Lear* are evil creatures whose deaths are appropriate rewards for their actions; their sister, Cordelia, the soul of goodness, is murdered unjustly.

8. In *Cymbeline,* Imogen, Guiderius (Polydore), and Arviragus (Cadwal) are all children of King Cymbeline, but do not discover their relationship until the final act.

9. Claudio is imprisoned for impregnating Juliet in *Measure for Measure.* His sister, Isabella, pleads for his life.

10. In *Troilus and Cressida,* Troilus and his brothers, Deiphobus, Hector, and Helenus, risk their lives in war for their brother Paris's love of Helen.

11. In *Titus Andronicus,* Saturninus becomes an emperor, but his brother Bassianus gets the girl—briefly.

12. Katherine in *The Taming of the Shrew* is described as "curst," at the beginning of the play, but is tamed after her wedding to Petruchio. On the other hand, her sister Bianca, who is sweet and agreeable while being courted, becomes much less tractable after her marriage.

13. Don John the Bastard fomented a rebellion against his brother Don Pedro, but once he is vanquished, he is forgiven by Don Pedro. Still, he would like to get even with his brother in *Much Ado About Nothing.*

14.These two royal brothers, Henry, Prince of Wales, and John of Lancaster, fight bravely in *1 Henry IV, 2 Henry IV,* and *Henry V.*

15. In *Hamlet,* Laertes and Ophelia are sad when he returns to Paris.

Pericles

16. b. Pericles comes from Tyre, a Phoenician city, on the coast of what is now Lebanon. It was founded at the start of the third millennium B.C., experienced a golden age in the tenth century B.C, and was conquered by Alexander in 332 B.C., about a hundred years before the date of Shakespeare's play.

17. a. Pericles has heard great praise of the daughter of Antiochus, is immediately aflame with desire when he sees her, and ready to love her passionately.

18. c. Helicanus is one of the lords of the play, and Pericles's adviser.

19. b. Antiochus wants to murder Pericles because Pericles solves the riddle and correctly ascertains that Antiochus and his daughter have had incestuous relations.

20. b. In Tarsus, the people are starving. Pericles comes with ships loaded with corn, which he gives generously.

21. b. The fishermen are equally generous with Pericles, and happy to provide food and clothes, and to turn over his armor when it is dragged out of the sea.

22. a. Thaisa writes her father that she will "wed the stranger knight,/Or never more to view nor day nor light" (II.v.16–17), which is exactly what her father also wishes.

23. a. Thaisa supposedly dies in childbirth, on shipboard (III.i).

24. c. Pericles then puts her in a coffin with spices and jewels, and the sailors cast her overboard because they superstitiously believe that the storm will not cease until the ship is "cleared of the dead" (III.i.49).

25. c. Antiochus and his daughter, while seated in a chariot, are slain by a fire from heaven that "came and shrivell'd up their bodies" (II.iv.7–10).

26. c. Although the period is not specific, Pericles roams the seas unhappily for sixteen years.

27. a. After leaving the baby Marina with Cleon and Dionyza, Pericles declares that he will not cut his hair until she is married (III.iii.29), but when he is told some years later that

she is dead, he vows never to "wash his face nor cut his hairs" (IV.iv.28).

28. b. Marina bests Philoten in all aspects: in weaving, sewing, singing, writing, so that Dionyza is consumed with envy and ready to kill Marina.

29. a. Marina manages to avoid losing her virginity in the brothel by converting her clients to a virtuous life (IV.v.3–10).

30. a. Marina so impresses the governor of Mytilene with her purity that he gives her enough gold so that she can convince the Bawd she will be more profitable as a teacher, because she can "sing, weave, sew, and dance" (IV.vi.194).

31. i. Marina's father seems a little slow to acknowledge his daughter. Perhaps he thinks she's just looking for a handout or is part of some Byzantine plot. But the "good palace guard" is fictional.

32. b. Thaisa becomes a vestal of Diana.

33. c. As Gower declares, in the last few lines of the play:

> "For wicked Cleon and his wife, when fame
> Had spread their cursed deed, the honour'd name
> Pericles, to rage the city turn,
> That him and his they in his palace burn;
> The gods for murder seemed so content
> To punish them; although not done, but meant."
>   (V.iii.95–100)

34. 1. a. Antiochus is the father of the No-Name Daughter.
    2. c. Cleon is the father of Philoten.
    3. b. Pericles is the father of Marina.
    4. d. Simonides is the father of Thaisa.

Mistakes and Mishaps

35. In *The Comedy of Errors,* the merchant Angelo gives the golden chain that Antipholus of Ephesus has ordered for his wife (then promised to the Courtesan) to Antipholus of Syracuse. The Courtesan has already given Antipholus of Ephesus a ring to trade for the chain and she is angry when he can't produce it. The error is not undone until the last scene of the play.

36. It is an accident that an illiterate servant of the house of Capulet in *Romeo and Juliet* runs into Romeo, who is able to read. When Romeo helps the servant by reading the guest list to the ball, he discovers that Rosaline, the girl he thinks he loves, has been invited, and he and his friends determine to crash the party (I.ii.).

37. In *Othello* Desdemona uses her handkerchief in an attempt to soothe Othello's brow. He pushes her arm away, and the handkerchief drops. In her concern for Othello, Desdemona is not aware of its loss (III.iii). Thereafter, Emilia picks it up and gives it to her husband, Iago, who plants it in Cassio's lodging, who, in turn, gives it to his girlfriend, Bianca, as Othello watches from a distance. Seeing the handkerchief in Cassio's hand, Othello is convinced that Desdemona is unfaithful.

38. Hamlet did not mean to kill Polonius, at least not then (III.iv.). He mistakenly thought he was killing Claudius, when he heard the voice behind the arras. Oh well.

39. Isn't it fortunate that Ragozin, the prisoner, dies of natural causes so that his head can be substituted for Claudio's in *Measure for Measure?*

40. In *Much Ado About Nothing,* a servant overhears a conversation in the garden that he mistakenly believes (and reports) to be the Prince confessing his love of Hero and his desire to tell her of it (I.ii). In actuality, the Prince is going to woo Hero for Claudio.

41. Puck makes a bad mistake in *A Midsummer Night's Dream* when he drops the love juice into Lysander's rather than Demetrius's eyes (II.ii.). Don't all Athenians look alike? Chaos results when Lysander wakes, rejects Hermia, and pursues Helena.

42. In *The Two Noble Kinsmen* Emilia must choose between Palamon and Arcite, both honorable young men. Their duel produces a winner in Arcite, and Emilia accepts him, leaving Palamon heartbroken, when word comes of a convenient accident: Arcite has been thrown from his horse and killed.

43. Coming upon him unexpectedly, Orlando in *As You Like It* is the savior of his brother, Oliver. The snake, seeing Orlando, slides away, and Orlando then does battle with the lioness, "who quickly fell before him" (IV.iii.132).

Cymbeline

44. c. Posthumus was born after his father's death; his father was surnamed Leonatus for the deeds he accomplished in the conflict against the Romans. Cymbeline named the baby, born as his mother died, Posthumus Leonatus.

45. b. The King's two sons were stolen by their nurse, at the urging of Morgan, who had been banished unjustly.

46. c. Posthumus has married the King's daughter, Imogen, and thus incurred Cymbeline's wrath.

47. a. Imogen and Posthumus exchange love tokens; she presents him with a diamond, he gives her a bracelet.

48. a. In Rome, Posthumus accepts the challenge of Iachimo, who says: "I will lay you ten thousand ducats to your ring . . . and will bring . . . that honour of hers which you imagine so reserved" (I.iv.138–43).

49. a. The Queen asks the doctor for a box of poisons.

50. b. The doctor provides her with drugs that "will stupefy and dull the sense awhile" (I.v.37).

51. a. Iachimo's attempt to seduce Imogen through lies about Posthumus is not successful, so he resorts to trickery to gain entrance to her bedroom.

52. e. Iachimo takes advantage of the sleeping Imogen to note the furnishings of her room (a); almost kisses her because she is so beautiful (c); manages to steal the bracelet (b); and thus has enough evidence to convince Posthumus of Imogen's infidelity (d).

53. a. Cloten plants musicians outside Imogen's bedchamber to sing "Hark, hark! the lark at heaven's gate sings" (II.iii.22), a morning song, in his attempt to win her.

54. a. Imogen says that Posthumus's "meanest garment" is dearer to her "than all the hairs above thee, / Were they all made such men" (II.iii.140–41). Thus the dim-witted Cloten finds a suit of Posthumus to wear.

55. b. Posthumus's outcry against women is a direct result of Iachimo's lies and trickery.

56. e. Imogen accepts the hospitality of Morgan and his sons (a), but feeling ill, takes the drug that Pisanio has given her, and falls into a stupor. The two sons of Belarius, Cadwal and Polydore, supposing Imogen dead, sing a beautiful mourning song (c) (IV.ii.258–80).

57. a. Cadwal and Polydore are really Arviragus and Guiderius, the sons of Cymbeline.

58. a. When Imogen awakes from her stupor, she believes the headless man next to her is Posthumus, since he is in Posthumus's clothes.

59. b. When Posthumus appears again, he is fighting for the Romans.

60. a. He realizes that he is fighting for the wrong side and deserts the Romans.

61. d. The dream sequence shows that the prophecy is fulfilled (a), provides great fortune to Posthumus (b), and also shows that Jupiter has hovered over him since his birth (c).

62. g. The doctor Cornelius reports that the Queen confessed that she "abhorr'd" Cymbeline (b), wanted to poison Imogen (d), and repented only that "the evils she hatch'd were not effected; so / Despairing died" (e) (V.v.59–60).

63. a. As Imogen attempts to reveal herself to Posthumus, he strikes her, saying, "Thou scornful page, / There lie thy part" (V.v.228–29).

64. a. Iachimo produces the ring he supposedly won from Posthumus and also the bracelet he stole from Imogen while she was sleeping.

65. c. In the final scene, Cymbeline is reunited with his daughter, his two sons, and his son-in-law.

66. b. Although the statement of the play is "Pardon's the word to all" (V.v.422), the only one requiring pardon here is Iachimo.

Lovers and Lunatics

67. Jessica, in *The Merchant of Venice,* steals a casket containing gold, jewels, and the turquoise ring, dresses herself as a boy, and elopes with Lorenzo (II.vi.).

68. This is Valentine in *The Two Gentlemen of Verona,* betrayed by Proteus, his treacherous friend, and banished.

69. In *Othello,* Roderigo gives Iago money and jewels to plead his case with Desdemona, and in act 4, scene ii, when he says he wants his jewels back, Iago plots against his life.

70. Sir Andrew Aguecheek, in *Twelfth Night*, is encouraged by Sir Toby Belch to woo his niece Olivia, although she seems uninterested.

71. In *Richard III,* Richard woos Lady Anne as she is following the casket containing her murdered father-in-law, Henry VI. His wooing apparently successful, he says, at the end of the scene, "Was ever woman in this humour woo'd?/Was ever woman in this humour won?/I'll have her; but I will not keep her long" (I.ii.228–30).

72. Iachimo, in *Cymbeline,* wagers with Posthumus about the faithfulness of his wife, Imogen. His trickery almost works, but Posthumus and Imogen are eventually reunited.

73. In *The Tempest,* Ferdinand falls in love with Miranda. Prospero, her father, does not want the courtship to be too easy, so he sets certain tasks for Ferdinand.

74. Helena, in *All's Well That Ends Well,* loves Bertram, the Count Rousillon. He will not accept her until she gets a certain ring from his finger and provides proof she's been in bed with him. She does.

75. Falstaff woos "both high and low, both rich and poor," and in this instance he is trying to woo Mistress Ford in *The Merry Wives of Windsor.* But Pistol warns Ford, the encounter is interrupted, and Falstaff escapes with the laundry (III.iii).

76. Claudio and Hero are fast smitten with each other in *Much Ado About Nothing.* But Don John plots against them and the marriage doesn't happen until Claudio is properly remorseful for his lack of trust.

77. In *As You Like It,* Rosalind encounters Orlando, who has been pasting bad poetry about his love for her on trees. She takes him on as a pupil, ostensibly to "cure him" of this madness, but she is really testing his love for her.

78. This is Florizel, in *The Winter's Tale,* the wooer of Perdita, the daughter of a shepherd. When his father discovers the courtship, he is furious, and the two lovers must flee.

79. Everyone knows this is Romeo, one of the "star-crossed lovers," rash in his actions but true in his love.

80. So speaks Othello, the much-honored general of the Venetians, who falls in love with the much sought-after young beauty of Venice.

81. Berowne and his friends in *Love's Labor's Lost* take the silly vow, immediately break it, and then are much relieved to be enabled to woo their ladies enthusiastically

The Winter's Tale

82. b. Sixteen years elapse between the first three acts of the play and last two.

83. a. The first act of the play takes place in Sicilia, Leontes' kingdom.

84. c. Polixenes has been a guest at Leontes' castle for "nine changes of the wat'ry star" (I.ii.1), but let's not leap to conclusions.

85. b. Leontes accuses Hermione of having an affair with Polixenes and accuses her of bearing his child. He also suspects that Mamillius is not his son.

86. a. Camillo tries to defend Hermione, but when he sees that it is useless, he tells Leontes that he believes him and "will fetch off Bohemia for't" (I.ii.334).

87. e. In a fury, Leontes tells Antigonus first to "take it hence / And see it instantly consum'd with fire" (II.iii.133–34), and then to "bear it / To some remote and desert place . . . and that there thou leave it" (II.iii.176–77).

88. d. When the message from the Oracle is read, Leontes at first denies the truth of it, but when a servant enters with news of Mamillius's death, and Hermione swoons, Leontes suddenly confesses his misdeeds and begs pardon of Apollo (III.ii).

89. b. Paulina functions as Leontes' conscience, insisting that he acknowledge the past and understand that the consequences of some deeds are irrevocable.

90. a. Antigonus is eaten by a bear in act 3, scene 3, as is graphically described by the Clown.

91. b. Time appears as a character with an hourglass, which he turns to allow the grains to run the other way and admits, as he skips over sixteen years, that he has the ability to "please some" and "try all" (IV.i.1).

92. b. Polixenes is annoyed with Florizel for the amount of time Florizel has spent at the shepherd's house and decides that he will "have some question with the shepherd" (IV.ii.54).

93. a. One of the motifs of the play is the passage of time, roughly the passage of a generation, which allows a baby to mature.

94. b. Autolycus, the rogue, says he sells just about everything. The one item he does not enumerate, however, is snuffboxes; however, if pressed, he could probably produce one from a back pocket somewhere (IV.iv).

95. b. Perdita and Polixenes differ in their opinions of horticulture. Perdita does not plant anything that has been artificially bred and prefers to depend upon nature alone; Polixenes claims that intentional breeding of flowers is an art and adds to nature (IV.iv.84–97).

96. a. Florizel and Perdita, to receive a friendly welcome in Sicilia from Polixenes, lie about their reason for being there.

97. Score a point if you answer all correctly.

    a. False. Mamillius remains dead.

    b. True. Perdita and Florizel are to be married.

    c. False. The restored Hermione forgives the changed Leontes.

    d. True. Polixenes and Leontes renew their boyhood friendship.

    e. True. Paulina is to marry Camillo.

98. 1. e. savory
    2. b. lavender
    3. d. marjoram
    4. c. marigold

Admittedly, this was a tough one. The passage reads:

> "Here's flow'rs for you,
> Hot *lavender,* mints, *savory, marjoram,*
> The *marigold,* that goes to bed with th' sun
> And with him rises weeping."

Adjectives

Shakespeare's adjectival choices are astonishing. Here are the complete passages:

99. "Now is the winter of our discontent
    Made *glorious* summer by this sun of York."
                     (Richard III, I.i.1–2)

100. "O what a rogue and *peasant* slave am I."
                      (Hamlet, II.ii.576)

101.   "She never told her love,
    But let concealment, like a worm i' the bud,
    Feed on her *damask* cheek."
              (Twelfth Night, II.iv.113–15)

102.　　　　"Yet I'll not shed her blood,
　　Nor scar that *whiter* skin of hers than snow,
　　And smooth as *monumental* alabaster."
　　　　　　　　　　　　　　　(*Othello* V.ii.3–5)

103. "From forth the *fatal* loins of these two foes
　　A pair of *star-cross'd* lovers take their life."
　　　　　　　　　(*Romeo and Juliet,* Prologue.5–6)

104.　　　　　　　　　"Present fears
　　Are less than *horrible* imaginings"
　　　　　　　　　　　(*Macbeth,* I.iii.137–38)

105. "As flies to *wanton* boys are we to the gods,
　　They kill us for their sport."
　　　　　　　　　　(*King Lear,* IV.i.38–39)

106. "I am a very *foolish,* fond old man."
　　　　　　　　　　　(*King Lear,* IV.vii.60)

107. "Age cannot wither her, nor custom stale
　　Her *infinite* variety."
　　　　　　　(*Antony and Cleopatra,* II.ii.240–41)

108.　　　　"O *brave, new* world,
　　That has such people in't!"
　　　　　　　　　(*The Tempest,* V.i.184–85)

109.–116. "There is a devil haunts thee in the likeness of an old fat man, a tun of man is thy companion. Why dost thou converse with that trunk of humours, that *bolting-hutch* of beastliness, that *swollen* parcel of dropsies, that *huge* bombard of sack, that *stuffed* cloak-bag of guts, that *roasted* Manningtree ox with the pudding in his belly, that *reverend* vice, that *grey* iniquity, that *father* ruffian, that vanity in years?"
　　　　　　　　　　(*1 Henry IV,* II.iv.492–98)

117. "Thus far, with rough and *all-unable* pen,
　　Our *bending* author hath pursu'd the story."
　　　　　　　　　(*Henry V,* Epilogue 1–2)

The Tempest

118. c. Prospero was ousted from his dukedom by his brother Antonio, who raised an army while Prospero studied and neglected his political duties.

119. b Although Prospero and his daughter, Miranda, were cast to sea in a rotten hulk of a boat, the loyal lord Gonzalo provided them with food, clothes, and books.

120. c. The witch Sycorax confined Ariel in a cloven pine for a dozen years because Ariel was "too delicate / To act her earthy and abhorr'd commands" (I.ii.273–74). (We can only imagine what they were!)

121. c. Prospero promises Ariel his freedom "after two days" (I.ii.298).

Ariel has dispersed the shipwrecked company into three groups:

122. I. d. Ferdinand has been left alone.

123. II. a. Adrian, b. Alonzo, c. Antonio, e. Francisco, f. Gonzalo, and g. Sebastian

124. III. h. Stephano and i. Trinculo

125. b. Prospero enslaved Caliban because he tried to rape Miranda.

126. b. The task that Prospero sets Ferdinand is to pile up logs.

127. a. Stephano has ridden to shore on a butt of sack and has enjoyed its contents ever since.

128. c. The plot of Sebastian and Antonio to murder Alonzo is foiled by Ariel, who sings in Gonzalo's ear and awakens him (II.i).

129. a. Caliban is very certain that the only way to kill Prospero is "First to possess his books; for without them /

He's but a sot, as I am, nor hath not/One spirit to command"
(III.ii.100–102).

130. c. The function of the masque is to celebrate the lovers'
virtue and to bless the marriage.

131. c. The purpose of the "glistering apparel" is to lure the
two conspirators, with their accomplice Caliban, into a trap, so
they can be rounded up.

132. False. Caliban seems to have a moment of repentance
and says that he will "be wise hereafter/And seek for grace"
(V.i.294–95).

133. True. The marriage of Ferdinand and Miranda is ap-
plauded by both fathers.

134. False. Prospero will return to Milan and resume his position as Duke.

135. True. Ariel is freed.

136. False. Prospero forgives Antonio.

137. c. All but c are statements made by scholars of Shakespeare. The first (a) is by Frank Kermode and was quoted in a
publication of the *Stratford Ontario School Newsletter* of 1976.
The second quotation (b) is from a review of Christine Dym-
kowski's book *Shakespeare in Performance: The Tempest* by
Michael D. Friedman (*Shakespeare Quarterly,* Winter 2001,
530). The last passage (d) is from an article by Curt Breight
entitled "'Treason doth never prosper': *The Tempest* and the
Discourse of Treason" (*Shakespeare Quarterly,* Spring, 1990,
1). The third passage (c) is just gobbledygook.

The Two Noble Kinsmen

138. a. John Fletcher (1579–1625) is believed to have been
Shakespeare's collaborator, as he probably also was for *Henry
VIII* and the lost *Cardenio*.

139. c. Boccaccio's *Teseida*, of two brothers who fight over the same woman, is a possible source; Chaucer's *The Knight's Tale* is acknowledged as a source in Gower's opening Prologue. Ovid was no help.

140. b. Palamon and Arcite are cousins, and nephews to King Creon.

141. b. The Three Queens come before Theseus and beg him to recover their husbands' bodies. The men were slain by Creon and left in the fields, where he refuses to allow the women to "burn their bones [or]/To urn their ashes" (I.i.43–44).

142. a. Palamon and Arcite want to leave Thebes because they view Creon as a tyrant and decide to leave the court, that "we may nothing share/Of his loud infamy"(I.ii.75–76).

143. c. In prison, Palamon says, "I do not think it possible our friendship/Should ever leave us." Arcite replies, "And after death our spirits shall be led/To those that love eternally" (II.ii.114–17), but when Emilia enters the garden, these vows are toast.

144. c. The Jailer's Daughter is betrayed by her own fantasies about Palamon, which lead her into madness.

145. a. Despite their protestations of love for one another, when it comes down to the girl, Palamon and Arcite are ready to square off.

146. b. Before the duel, Arcite prays to Mars for military skill so that he will be "styled the lord o'th'day" (V.i.60). Mars replies with a great clanging of armor and the sounds of battle.

147. c. Palamon prays to Venus, the goddess of love, and begs for a sign of her favor. He is rewarded with the sounds of music and the fluttering of doves' wings (V.1).

148. c. At the end of the play, the Jailer's Daughter will marry the Wooer, whom she believes is Palamon. Palamon and his

knights, perhaps out of sympathy for her mental affliction, provide money for her dowry.

149. a. At the end of the play Emilia is won by Palamon, since the horse that she gave to Arcite conveniently throws him to his death, thus solving the dilemma of her choice.

150. c. According to the *Riverside Shakespeare*, "the characters move from a state of innocence, which is presexual, into an area of experience where the will seems totally irrelevant to the way things will turn out" (1641).

Bard Buster I

151. h. The author of *A Groatsworth of Wit* is Robert Greene, who declared that Shakespeare was an "upstart crow," with "a tiger's hart wrapt in a Player's hide."

152. o. Shakespeare the deerslayer appears in Nicholas Rowe's preface to his 1709 edition of his works, where the story goes that Shakespeare had some rowdy friends who enticed him into the business of deer stealing on the estate belonging to Sir Thomas Lucy of Charlecote.

153. k. Dr. John Hall married his daughter Susanna, becoming Shakespeare's son-in-law.

154. t. William Pembroke was the third Earl of Pembroke (the Lord Chamberlain) and one of the dedicatees of the First Folio.

155. x. Will Kempe was the principal comedian of Shakespeare's company before 1599, when he had an argument and left the company.

156. n. Sir William Davenant's play was called *Law Against Lovers*.

157. e. The principal tragedian of Shakespeare's company was Richard Burbage, who originated the roles of Hamlet, Lear, and Macbeth, among others.

158. m. From 1592 to 1606 Philip Henslowe maintained a diary, an exact account of his dealings with London theater companies, which is the most valuable document existing today of Elizabethan stage history.

159. p. John Manningham, a law student of the Middle Temple, kept a diary with several anecdotes about Shakespeare; he also helped to establish a date for a performance of *Twelfth Night* (February 2, 1602).

160. c. Shakespeare's mother's maiden name was Mary Arden (but you knew that).

161. f. *Cardenio*, now lost, was reputed to be by Shakespeare and Fletcher.

162. w. Francis Collins was Shakespeare's attorney and helped with his real estate investments and with his will.

163. s. Edward de Vere was the seventeenth Earl of Oxford.

164. j. *A Groatsworth of Wit* contains the first allusion to Shakespeare in London.

165. g. Sir William Davenant—whose father ran a tavern—called the Cross Inn on the way to Stratford-upon-Avon, perpetuated the story that Shakespeare had stopped for more than drink there, and that thus he was Shakespeare's bastard son.

166. d. Robert Armin joined Shakespeare's company in 1600 after Will Kempe left.

167. v. Nicholas Rowe was Shakespeare's first biographer, gathering material for "Some Account of the Life &s. of Mr William Shakespear" (1709), which prefaced his edition to *The Works of Shakespeare.*

168. r. Francis Meres was the author of *Palladis Tamia,* a book of criticism that lists twelve of Shakespeare's plays, perhaps all that he knew at that time—1597–98.

169. u. *The Puritan Widow* was included in the Third Folio but was not by Shakespeare.

170. l. Shakespeare's wife was Anne Hathaway (but that was too easy).

Bard Buster II

171. In *The Two Gentlemen of Verona*, Valentine flees to Mantua when Sylvia's father discovers their plans to elope and banishes him.

172. The seven women who disguise themselves as men are

    a. Julia in *The Two Gentlemen of Verona*
    b. Portia in *The Merchant of Venice*
    c. Nerissa in *The Merchant of Venice*
    d. Jessica in *The Merchant of Venice*
    e. Rosalind in *As You Like It*
    f. Imogen in *Cymbeline*
    g. Viola in *Twelfth Night*

173. The American actor-director who spearheaded the restoration of the Globe is Sam Wanamaker (1919–1993).

174. a. January 6 is "Twelfth Night" and represents the end of the Christmas festivities. Shakespeare's *Twelfth Night,* the last of his festive comedies, bears no relation to the actual date.

    b. March 15 is the Ides of March, the date on which Caesar was assassinated, so it looms importantly in *Julius Caesar.*

    c. Two weeks before Lammastide, August 1, is the date Juliet will be fourteen, according to her nurse (I.iii.21).

    d. June 21–24 is considered midsummer, and as Theseus, in *A Midsummer Night's Dream,* says, there are four days until his marriage to Hippolyta.

    e. October 25 is St. Crispin's Day, and the day of the Battle of Agincourt in *Henry V.*

175. c. Several accounts, possibly apocryphal, cite Shakespeare's playing Hamlet's Ghost as well as Adam in *As You Like*

It. There is no mention of his playing Richard in *Richard III,* although his colleague Richard Burbage certainly did.

176. The name of the actor who played Othello over three thousand times is Vagram Papazian, an Armenian.

177. In *Ran,* the major change Kurosawa made in the cast of characters was to change the three daughters to sons. No Japanese feudal lord would have been influenced by daughters as in Shakespeare's original.

178. Here are the adaptations:

   a. *Sauny the Scot* was *A Midsummer Night's Dream.*
   b. *The History and Fall of Caius Marcius* was *Coriolanus.*
   c. *The Enchanted Island* was *The Tempest.*
   d. *Love Betrayed; or The Agreeable Disappointment* was *Twelfth Night.*
   e. *The Injured Princess* was *Cymbeline.*
   f. *The Universal Passion* was *Much Ado About Nothing.*
   g. *Love in a Forest* was *As You Like It.*

179. The actor who defended his pathetic performance as Hamlet in 1878 with a net across the stage was George Jones, who called himself Count Johannes.

180. The gentleman, whose noble intentions earned him the curses of farmers across the country, was Eugene Schieffelin. He belonged to the American Acclimatization Society, which sought to introduce interesting European varieties of plants and animals to this country. Schieffelin's aim was to introduce Shakespeare's birds; and unfortunately, the starling took hold in Central Park and proliferated throughout the country. It really did not fit the category of an "interesting variety," as it is an aggressive bird, chasing off the smaller birds, nor did it add to the legend of Shakespeare's environmental concerns. Although he mentions many birds from the nightingale to the sparrow, the starling is mentioned only once, in *1 Henry IV* (I.iii.222–24), and then derogatorily.

Epilogue

Congratulations! You deserve all sorts of praise and kudos if you've managed to navigate these 723 questions from Amateurs through Superstars. If you knew 400 of the answers the first time through, you deserve even more praise—and disbelief.

If you didn't, perhaps you'll be encouraged to visit a Shakespeare festival, or your neighborhood theater, or to read one or more of the plays.

But acknowledge this: you could be perfect on all of these quizzes, have seen hundreds of productions, be able to recognize every allusion in every advertisement, television commercial, and newspaper editorial, and think that you have plucked out the heart of his mystery, but you haven't beaten the Bard. Like existence itself, Shakespeare will always be a mystery. "Let it be."